Joyce, Imperialism, & Postcolonialism

Irish Studies
James MacKillop, *Series Editor*

Other titles in Irish Studies

Catholic Emancipations: Irish Fiction from Thomas Moore to James Joyce
Emer Nolan

Grand Opportunity: The Gaelic Revival and Irish Society, 1893–1910
Timothy G. McMahon

An Irish Literature Reader: Poetry Prose, Drama, 2d. ed.
Maureen O'Rourke Murphy and James MacKillop, eds.

Irish Orientalism: A Literary and Intellectual History
Joseph Lennon

Joyce and Reality: The Empirical Strikes Back
John Gordon

Joyce and the City: The Significance of Place
Michael Begnal, ed.

Joyce and the Joyceans
Morton P. Levitt, ed.

Of Irish Descent: Origin Stories, Genealogy, and the Politics of Belonging
Catherine Nash

Party Pieces: Oral Storytelling and Social Performance in Joyce and Beckett
Alan W. Friedman

Twentieth-Century Irish Drama: Mirror up to Nation
Christopher Murray

Joyce, Imperialism, & Postcolonialism

EDITED BY

Leonard Orr

SYRACUSE UNIVERSITY PRESS

Syracuse, New York 13244-5160

First Edition 2008
08 09 10 11 12 13 6 5 4 3 2 1

Chapter 6, "What's Wrong with Hybridity: The Impotence of Postmodern Political Ideals in *Ulysses* and *Midnight's Children*," by Michael Tratner, first appeared in *In-Between: Essays and Studies in Literary Criticism* (New Delhi) 12, no. 1/2 (2003): 113–25.

The paper used in this publication meets the minimum requirements of American National Standard for Information Sciences—Permanence of Paper for Printed Library Materials, ANSI Z39.48–1984.∞™

For a listing of books published and distributed by Syracuse University Press, visit our Web site at SyracuseUniversityPress.syr.edu.

ISBN-13: 978-0-8156-3188-0 ISBN-10: 0-8156-3188-X

Library of Congress Cataloging-in-Publication Data
Joyce, imperialism, and postcolonialism / edited by Leonard Orr. — 1st ed.
p. cm. — (Irish studies)
Includes bibliographical references and index.
ISBN 978-0-8156-3188-0 (cloth : alk. paper) 1. Joyce, James, 1882–1941—Criticism and interpretation. 2. Politics and literature—Ireland—History—20th century. 3. Imperialism in literature. 4. Postcolonialism in literature. 5. Identity (Psychology) in literature. 6. Ireland—In literature. I. Orr, Leonard, 1953–
PR6019.O9Z6646 2008
823'.912—dc22

Manufactured in the United States of America

Contents

Illustrations

Acknowledgments

THIS BOOK has been in the planning and mulling-over stage for a long time. After I edited *Yeats and Postmodernism* (Syracuse University Press, 1991), with a number of political and New Historicist reassessments of Yeats's work, it seemed that it would be fruitful to work in the same way with Joyce. But there was a sudden flood of works in the 1990s that were looking at Joyce with a bewildering range of political and historical lenses (Marx, Foucault, Frankfurt School, Antonio Gramsci, Bakhtin, feminist and gender analyses, popular culture and mass movements, particular historical events, and extraliterary European contexts). But Joyce (and Ireland itself) has had a problematic and difficult place within the relatively recent development of imperial and postcolonial studies.

A few years ago, I chaired a seminar at the meeting of the Modernist Studies Association on "Modernism and Post-Colonialism." No authors or countries were mentioned in the call for seminar participants, so I was amazed to see that almost all of the seminar papers were on Joyce, sometimes in connection with other well-established postcolonial novelists. This was intriguing and led to a discussion that continued beyond the boundaries of the seminar or that MSA meeting to wrestle with Joyce, Beckett, Yeats, and other authors in the context of the burgeoning theoretical writings on Irish colonialism and postcolonialism.

In developing this book, I would like to thank, first of all, the contributors of the essays, all written specifically for this volume, for their wonderful work, flexibility, and goodwill. I know they all took time from their other research projects to contribute to the volume. Other people discussed or corresponded with me about the volume and I am happy for their ideas and encouragement. I want to thank Christopher GoGwilt, Enda Duffy, Zack

Bowen, Srinavas Aravamudan, Marjorie Howes, Thomas Hofheinz, James Fairhall, David Spurr, M. Keith Booker, and David Lloyd. My daughter, Leah Orr, was especially helpful for her meticulous work as a research assistant for the volume. Finally, I want to thank the editors and staff of Syracuse University Press for their enthusiasm and support of this project from my first proposal of the collection on to the present.

Contributors

CHRISTY L. BURNS earned her Ph.D. at the Johns Hopkins Humanities Center. She is currently an associate professor of English at the College of William and Mary, teaching also in Women's Studies and Film Studies. Her first book, *Gestural Politics: Stereotype and Parody in Joyce,* appeared in 2000, and she has published articles on Irish studies, nationalism, gender, and sexuality issues in modern and postmodern literature. In media and film studies, she has published on postmodern paranoia in *The X-Files* and on race and color-blindness critique in the film, *Suture.* Most recently, she has published on Irish film and globalization (in *Global Babel*). Her current book project addresses the role of sensate experience in modern to contemporary fiction.

JON HEGGLUND is currently an assistant professor of English at Washington State University, where he teaches courses in twentieth-century British and Anglophone literatures, film studies, and literary theory. He has published on Forster, Joyce, Graham Greene, and "imperial" Hollywood films of the 1930s. He is finishing a book manuscript on the intersection between literary and geographical representations in early twentieth-century discourses of globalization.

WILLIAM C. MOTTOLESE has taught at Fordham University and Saint Joseph's College in Indiana and is presently co-chair of the English Department at Convent of the Sacred Heart in Connecticut. He leads a *Ulysses* discussion group for the James Joyce Society in New York City and serves on the faculty of the Mercantile Library in Manhattan. He has published on such subjects as Olaudah Equiano, Laurence Sterne, and James Joyce and is presently at work on a book manuscript on James Joyce and ethnography.

EUGENE O'BRIEN is senior lecturer, head of the English Department and director of the Mary Immaculate College Irish Studies Centre in Mary Immaculate College, Limerick. He has published five books to date on critical theory and Irish Studies, and has co-edited two collections on Franco-Irish Studies. He is editor of the *Contemporary Irish Writers and Filmmakers* series (Liffey Press) and of Edwin Mellen Press's *Studies in Irish Literature* and *Irish Studies* series and of the *Irish Book Review*.

LEONARD ORR is the Lewis E. and Stella G. Buchanan Distinguished Professor of English at Washington State University and the academic director of the Liberal Arts. He has written or edited many books including *Yeats and Postmodernism, A Dictionary of Critical Theory, A Joseph Conrad Companion, Critical Essays on Samuel Taylor Coleridge, Problems and Poetics of the Nonaristotelian Novel,* and *Don DeLillo's White Noise: A Reader's Guide.* Currently he is pursuing interdisciplinary research and teaching in the area of representations of the Holocaust and this has led to studying genocide, trauma and memory (as represented in literature, film, and art), and diaspora and exile literature.

ALLAN H. SIMMONS is reader in English literature at St. Mary's University College, Strawberry Hill. Author of *Joseph Conrad* (2006) for Palgrave and *Heart of Darkness* for Continuum (2007), he edited the Centennial Edition of *The Nigger of the "Narcissus"* for Everyman (1997) and co-edited *Lord Jim: Centennial Essays* (2000) and *Nostromo: Centennial Essays* (2004) for Rodopi of Amsterdam. Currently editing *Conrad in Context* for Cambridge University Press, he is general editor of *The Conradian: The Journal of the Joseph Conrad Society* (United Kingdom).

MICHAEL TRATNER is the Mary E. Garrett Alumnae Professor of English at Bryn Mawr College. He is the author of *Deficits and Desires: Economics and Literature in the Twentieth Century* (Stanford University Press, 2001) and *Modernism and Mass Politics: Joyce, Woolf, Eliot, Yeats* (Stanford University Press, 1995). He has a new book coming out soon entitled *Crowd Scenes: Movies and Mass Politics.*

TREVOR WILLIAMS is emeritus professor of English at the University of Victoria, B.C. He has published *Reading Joyce Politically* (University Press of Florida, 1997) and is working on a book aimed specifically at those who want to know the "relevance" of Joyce today.

Abbreviations for Works by Joyce

CW *The Critical Writings.* Edited by Ellsworth Mason and Richard Ellmann. New York: Viking, 1959.

D *Dubliners.* London: Secker and Warburg, 1994.

FW *Finnegans Wake.* New York: Viking, 1939; London: Faber and Faber, 1939. Subsequent editions have the same pagination.

Letters *Letters of James Joyce.* Vol. 1 edited by Stuart Gilbert. New York: Viking: 1957; reissued with corrections, 1966. Vols. 2 and 3 edited by Richard Ellmann. New York: Viking Press, 1966.

P *A Portrait of the Artist as a Young Man.* London: Jonathan Cape, 1985.

P-B *A Portrait of the Artist as a Young Man.* Edited by R. B. Kershner. Boston: Bedford Books/St. Martin's Press, 1993.

U *Ulysses.* Edited by Hans Walter Gabler. New York: Random House, 1986; London: Bodley Head, 1986. This edition includes chapter numbers and line numbers (i.e., 12.700 would be "Cyclops," line 700).

U-ML *Ulysses.* New York: Modern Library, 1961.

Joyce, Imperialism, & Postcolonialism

From High-Modern Aesthete to Postcolonial Subject

An Introduction to the Political Transformation of Joyce Studies

LEONARD ORR

IT WILL SURPRISE MOST READERS to note how recent the concept of a political Joyce is. Traditional Joyce critics of the 1950s through 1970s treated Joyce as either entirely disinterested in politics or having only a superficial understanding matters outside of literature and aesthetics. Admittedly, this was often built upon Joyce's own dismissive or sarcastic comments, but it accumulated into received wisdom. There are only a handful of passages in Richard Ellmann's authoritative biography dealing with Joyce's political ideas, even in the nearly nine hundred pages of the 1982 revised edition. Ellmann summarizes the political meandering of Joyce up to the time he left Ireland in 1904 in this way:

> He needed a redistribution of wealth if he was to be a spendthrift, and attended occasional meetings of a socialist group in Henry Street where prophets of the new day milder than Marx were discussed. The anarchist theories of the American Benjamin Tucker also attracted him for a time. Finally, he came to know the writings of Nietzsche, "that strong enchanter" whom Yeats and other Dubliners were discovering. . . . At heart Joyce can scarcely have been a Nietzschean any more than he was a socialist. (Ellmann 1982, 142)

Observing Ireland in 1907 from Italy, Joyce states his support for the Nationalist Sinn Féin movement, especially the boycotting of British goods to achieve economic and political independence. Ellmann personalizes and aestheticizes this by adding, "just as Joyce, abroad, would achieve the necessary artistic independence for his countrymen to import" (238). When World War I begins, Joyce is presented mocking all forms of government and was "supremely indifferent to the result and, so long as gunfire could not be heard, to the conflict itself" (383; see also 446). In Paris in 1932, he refused to be the guest of honor at a St. Patrick's Day party because the Irish ambassador would be there and Joyce did not want to seem to endorse the establishment of the Irish Republic (643n). In October 1939, with the Second World War just beginning, Joyce thought there was no reason or purpose for the war. "What was worse, it was distracting the world from reading *Finnegans Wake,* in which the unimportance of wars in the total cycle of human activity was made perfectly clear" (728).

Joyce was consistent in his conversation and essays on the necessity of the writer maintaining a distance from political ends and motives. In one of his earliest articles, "The Day of the Rabblement" (1901; censored by the faculty advisor of a University College Dublin student magazine, and published at his own expense), nineteen-year-old Joyce wrote, "If an artist courts the favour of the multitude he cannot escape the contagion of its fetichism *[sic]* and deliberate self-deception, and if he joins in a popular movement he does so at his own risk. Therefore, the Irish Literary Theatre by its surrender to the trolls has cut itself adrift from the line of advancement" (Joyce 1959, 71). The thematic motifs that emerge from Joyce's acerbic or aloof remarks about Ireland and its politics, especially in connection to Home Rule and its relationship to the British Empire, is that of betrayal, parochialism, repression, censorship, and intolerance.

Through most of the twentieth century, Joyce was the perfect type of the rootless and elite intellectual, apolitical and cosmopolitan. His fiction after *Dubliners* and *Portrait* seemed to confirm this. The disdain for Irish narrowness and intolerance went along with a call for world literature. In "The Day of the Rabblement," Joyce remarks that "A nation which never advanced so far as a miracle-play affords no literary model to the artist, and so he must look abroad. Earnest dramatists of the second rank, Sudermann, Björnson, and Giacosa, can write very much better plays than the Irish Literary Theatre has staged" (*CW,* 70). Even though all of Joyce's writing is set in

Ireland, it is as if this Ireland is entirely mythopoetic, like Nabokov's Zembla, Faulkner's Yoknapatawpha, or Hardy's Wessex. *Ulysses* and *Finnegans Wake,* in particular, in the eyes of most critics have transcended their specific and almost accidental time and place, and that is the greatest praise. In the beginning of his very influential *Reader's Guide to Finnegans Wake,* William York Tindall, one of the earliest teachers and disseminators of Joyce's fiction in the United States, notes that "*Finnegans Wake* is about anybody, anywhere, anytime" (Tindall 1969, 3).

But the issue of Joyce's political engagement is not so clear. Dominic Manganiello (1980) and Maria Tymoczko (1994) have demonstrated that during the period just prior to his leaving Ireland in October 1904, Joyce was engaged in all of the political debates, studied the Irish language (in a class taught by Patrick Pearse, one of the activists involved in the Easter Uprising in 1916). He read the popular newspapers such as the *United Irishman,* edited by the Sinn Féin leader Arthur Griffith. He was unusually well informed about traditional Irish-language literature, familiar with the best scholarly studies and translations available at the time as well as the translations published in the popular press. But he took no active part in Irish political causes. Joyce's intimates, such as his brother Stanislaus and his friend Arthur Power, considered him to have maintained socialist beliefs and sympathies, and he remained critical of both the pre–Civil War Irish politicians and the post–Irish Free State government leaders.

Joyce's movement out from Ireland was captured in the placing of cities and dates at the end of his novels: *A Portrait of the Artist as a Young Man* is signed "Dublin 1904/Trieste 1914." *Ulysses* closes with "Trieste-Zurich-Paris 1914–1921" and *Finnegans Wake* with "Paris 1922–1939." There are no returns to Dublin, although Dublin is always the setting of his work. He did not return when the Irish Free State was proclaimed at the end of 1922, and felt, no doubt correctly, that he would not be welcome in Ireland, and might even be in danger. His books were not officially available in Ireland, and he was largely either unknown or attacked by the Irish public. During his decade in Trieste, he wrote and lectured using the local dialect and was identified as Italian-Irish.

Colin MacCabe's 1978 *James Joyce and the Revolution of the Word* was one of the first works to try to demonstrate that Joyce's politics were central to the formation of his aesthetics and that the experimental techniques were themselves political and subversive. In his preface to the enlarged second edition, published in 2003, MacCabe recognizes some of the problems of his Marxist reading of the political Joyce. But MacCabe's work, in its focus on Joyce's outsider status whose work developed from his decolonization and refashioning of Ireland, has proven to be to be key for later Joyce studies. His book points out the directions of feminism, gender studies, and race in relationship to the colonial and postcolonial subject. MacCabe presents Joyce as outside the strictures of any of the existing nationalist political groups in Ireland and leaders (the Irish Republican Brotherhood, the Gaelic Athletic League, Arthur Griffith and Sinn Féin). Joyce could not follow the greatly increased political role of the Catholic Church in Ireland after the establishment of the Free State, which he saw in terms of repression and paralysis. Finally, MacCabe argues, in literature Joyce rejected the positions of both the Celtic Revivalists and the aesthetically reactionary audience and publishers of Ireland. Joyce's later apotheosis into the most obvious exemplar of high modernism seemed to remove him from political writing and effectiveness, as much as his physical self-exile removed him from Ireland. C. L. Innes points out that "Joyce and Yeats have both been appropriated as stars of the European and English modernist pantheon, and their writing has been acclaimed in proportion to the degree it can be tied and confined to aesthetic concerns, with an emphasis on reflexivity, self-containment and self-consciousness about the form and media of art, to the exclusion of political concerns" (Innes 2000a, 137).

In 1978, MacCabe was attempting to fill in the critical silence about Joyce's political beliefs. Part of this silence was because of the domination, on one hand, of formalist approaches in criticism, especially New Criticism, semiotics, and structuralism (and in later years Derridean and Lacanian poststructuralism). On the other hand, because of its innovative techniques and narrative difficulties, sexual openness, and lack of qualities required by socialist realism, Joyce's work had long been attacked by left-wing political critics as elitist and disengaged with reality.

MacCabe's work was followed by a handful of other books and articles focusing on Joyce's political and historically contexts (notably Dominic Manganiello's *Joyce's Politics* [1980] and Seamus Deane's *Celtic Revivals* [1985]).

But it was not until the 1990s, with the paradigm shift in critical theory to new historicism, cultural studies, and postcolonial studies (and more recently, globalization and literature, along with other interdisciplinary or transdisciplinary and transcultural approaches such as trauma studies and diaspora studies), that what had previously been denied or ignored became apparent (if still complex and contradictory). It was no longer possible to ignore the aspects of empire, colonialism, postcolonialism, nationalism, and constructions of race and gender in Joyce's work.

This turnaround in the situating of Joyce's work is all the more surprising because of the initial resistance toward treating Ireland as "postcolonial," although the Republic clearly is. Popular anthologies meant as textbooks, such as *The Arnold Anthology of Post-Colonial Literatures,* edited by John Thieme (1996), have sections on Africa, Australia, Canada, the Caribbean, New Zealand, South Pacific, and Asia, but ignore Ireland altogether. Most introductory books on the theory and practice of postcolonial criticism only have the briefest mentions of Ireland in the middle of larger discussions of race classifications and the replacement of indigenous language with the Imperial tongue (see virtually the same use of Ireland, for example, in *Key Concepts in Post-Colonial Studies,* by Bill Ashcroft, Gareth Griffiths, and Helen Tiffin, and *Colonialism/Postcolonialism,* by Ania Loomba, both published in 1998). None of these works mention Joyce at all.

This situation is reminiscent of the sudden entrance into Joyce studies in the mid-seventies (still dominated by formalistic criticism and allusion hunting) of deconstruction, Bakhtinian and Lacanian analyses, feminist criticism, and then gender studies. These approaches first appeared almost like guerilla actions, with handwritten signs at Joyce conferences inviting people who would be interested in such new areas of criticism applied to Joyce to meet in an unscheduled seminar in an unused conference room or a nearby restaurant. Once these approaches to Joyce's works were opened up, then it seemed obvious, clear, and, to varying degrees, persuasive. Joyce seemed the exemplary case for each of these newer approaches just as he now seems perfectly suited for postcolonial studies.

A full catalogue of the works that study Joyce's work through postcolonial perspectives in the single decade since 1994 is not possible here—it is such a full field—but a chronological skeleton includes James Fairhall's *James*

Joyce and the Question of History (1993); Maria Tymoczko's *The Irish Ulysses* (1994); Enda Duffy's *The Subaltern Ulysses* (1994); Vincent J. Cheng's *Joyce, Race, and Empire* (1995); Emer Nolan's *James Joyce and Nationalism* (1995); Thomas C. Hofheinz's *Joyce and the Invention of Irish History* (1995); the 1996 collection *Joyce and the Subject of History*, edited by Mark A. Wolleager, Victor Luftig, and Robert Spoo; Trevor L. Williams' *Reading Joyce Politically* (1997); Eugene O'Brien's *The Question of Irish Identity in the Writings of William Butler Yeats and James Joyce* (1998); Christine van Boheemen-Saaf's *Joyce, Derrida, Lacan and the Trauma of History* (1999b); the valuable collection edited by Derek Attridge and Marjorie Howes, *Semicolonial Joyce* (2000); M. Keith Booker's Ulysses, *Capitalism, and Colonialism* (2000); Christy L. Burns's *Gestural Politics* (2000); Andrew Gibson's *Joyce's Revenge* (2002a); David Spurr's *Joyce and the Scene of Modernity* (2003); Andras Ungar's *Joyce's* Ulysses *as National Epic* (2003); and the 2006 collection *Joyce, Ireland, Britain*, edited by Andrew Gibson and Len Platt. There were numerous other books that, though not focused on Joyce, provided further means of triangulating Joyce's writing and thought in the context of postcolonialism, such as David Lloyd's 1993 volume *Anomalous States*; Declan Kiberd's *Inventing Ireland* (1996); or the insightful collection of essays edited by Howard J. Booth and Nigel Rigby, *Modernism and Empire* (2000).

The works I have listed here, appearing over a fifteen-year time span, must stand to indicate numerous other books, dissertations, articles, collections of essays, and conference papers to illustrate the sea change that has overtaken Joyce studies. Joyce is no longer floating in the timeless, apolitical high modernist ether, the heavenly realm of literary monuments described by T. S. Eliot in "Tradition and the Individual Talent" where the great works coexist in eternal competition, nudging each other up and down when a new great work is created, but otherwise having no connection except to devoted and tireless exegetes. Although there are certainly focused formalist or nonpolitical studies of Joyce's works, they are presented to readers concerned with historical, social, and political contexts, unwilling to separate the texts from the world and author. A similar wave has overtaken many others in the modernist canon (Proust, Yeats, Beckett, Eliot, Pound, and so on; on Yeats, for example, see Ramazani 1998). This is not surprising; every new critical tool or approach developed since the 1920s has first been applied to Joyce's works by English-language critics and then applied to others.

The arguments that accompanied the early attempts to situate Joyce in the burgeoning field of postcolonial studies no longer need to be made, it would seem. Yet, the issues concerning Joyce have in many ways proliferated along with the maturing of postcolonialist scholarship. Where earlier Joyceans had stood firmly behind the notion, obvious and unequivocal, that Joyce held politics in contempt and disliked the Irish nationalists as much as he did the British imperialists, Joyceans now stand behind the notion of the politically committed, subversively anticolonial imperial subject in exile, the subaltern Joyce. A decade ago, Vincent J. Cheng said we have replaced the "canonical Joyce" with "postcolonial Joyce."

> One long-standing effect of this canonization—the elevation of an Irish-Catholic colonial writer like Joyce into the pantheon of the modernist greats—was rather insidious; it shifted attention away from the manifest political content and ideological discourse of Joyce's works by emphasizing his unarguably potent role and influence in stylistic revolution. . . . allowing us for decades to maintain a convenient blind spot when it comes to the political, wishing—like Gabriel Conroy—to believe that literature was above, and separate from, politics. (Cheng 1997, 81–82)

A similar process, though to a lesser extent, has occurred with other Irish writers, especially Yeats and Beckett. The postcolonial standings of these two writers are, of course, as complex as Joyce's own (see Esty 1999; Fleming 2001; Gjurgjan 1999; Martin-Iordache 2002; Meche 2000; Pearson 2001; Ramazani 1998; Regan 2000; Riquelme 1998; Said 1988). It is certainly worth noting that the same canonical figures of modernism, alone among Irish authors between the Celtic Twilight and Seamus Heaney and who were taken into the pantheon of European modernism, are now the authors who come to mind most immediately in Irish postcolonial literary criticism. The Irish writers most at odds with Ireland and its people, who wanted to transform it through aestheticization and spiritual magic, in the case of Yeats, or leave it permanently, in the case of Joyce and Beckett, are now seen to have been wrestling in fact with their political milieu and to have been subverting the empire through their visions, narrative and stylistic experiments, plots and characters, and explosion of language and meaning. Joyce, the emblematic high modernist, is now the perfect emblem of writing against the empire, especially with his most difficult, hermetic work, *Finnegans Wake*. David Spurr argues:

> The historical conditions of decolonization became one of the conditions for Joyce's last work, which makes decolonization into a discursive as well as an historical event. To read Joyce as a decolonized writer is to recognize that his historical perspective on the final stages of the imperial era coincides with his creation of a text which calls into question, formally and thematically, the structures of power from which writing is inherited. It is also to begin the process of rethinking Joyce's place in the context of European modernism, especially insofar as modernism has been held to represent a privileged aesthetic domain of an imperialist European society. (Spurr 1996, 872)

The awareness of this paradigm shift has made the scholars applying postcolonial notions to Joyce uneasy in a way that was not true for the decades of the canonical Joyce (even for people who have never read Joyce at all, according to many popular polls, *Ulysses* is the most important novel of the twentieth century). But Joyce's work was promoted by the other tenants of the modernist heaven: Eliot, Pound, and, in the next generation Nabokov and Beckett. The aesthetics and approaches that raised one to the heights raised them all. This is not the same situation for postcolonial studies, which might be seen to have its origins with Chinua Achebe, Gayatri Chakravorty Spivak, and Edward Said, speaking for the writing situation of Africa, India, and the Middle East. Postcolonial studies has been happily appropriated by American and European academics to be applied to European writers of particular situations of political exile and oppression: to Joyce, to Kafka, to Beckett, to Derrida and Jabès.

In response, a number of critics have argued against including Irish writers in the same category of "postcolonialism" as the writers situated in countries at a much greater distance from their European imperial oppressors. The discursive space now devoted to all of the analyses and arguments about the previously canonical modernist writers, they argue, is at the expense of their unknown, noncanonical, unanthologized authors. This is why we have had a proliferation of confusing categories. The term "white postcoloniality" has been used for authors such as Joyce or Katherine Mansfield who come from "national communities that are either European or of European racial origins" that "have historically existed within colonial conditions" (Majumdar 2007, 4; Majumdar notes that "White Postcolonials" was the title of a session at the MLA Convention in Philadelphia in 2004). Derek Attridge and Marjorie Howes made up the word "semicolonial" in the title of their collection of essays on Joyce in order to indicate his status as someone in a special boundary situation, part of European culture generally and British culture in particular, cosmopolitan and multilingual, but not in the "native" language and culture, not from the land but urban. Related to this is the question of whether Ireland itself qualifies to be considered "postcolonial" and, if so, when did that "post-" condition begin? (See Boehmer 1995; Carroll and King 2003; Lloyd 2001.)

Where is Joyce situated in the debates generated by postcolonial theory and discourse of the past decade? What are the useful concepts that have emerged in postcolonial theory that seem to be most fruitful to pursue with Joyce and his work (i.e., mimicry, appropriation, and hybridity)? The fictional situations and characters of his works arguably cover the widest possible range of colonial/postcolonial and imperialist postures and attitudes, and they use the full range of techniques associated with postcolonial literature. Joyce published most of his works as an expatriate during the time Ireland was a colony of the British Empire. The seventeen years of the writing of *Finnegans Wake* coincided with Ireland's civil war and independence. Is Joyce a postcolonial writer, a postimperial subject, or the colonized subject in exile? Is he a nationalist or an antinationalist or, perhaps, a disappointed revolutionary whose weapons of mass destruction are his increasingly experimental and "non-English" prose works? How does his work relate to postcolonial writers from other countries, languages, traditions, and colonial backgrounds? How is the modernist canon reshaped by postcolonial studies, or is it actually now recast and given new life by the current approach and exotic perspective? These are serious matters, and they have not yet been adequately answered or extended.

❧

The essays in this book take up many of these issues in different ways. Allan H. Simmons, in "Topography and Transformation: A Postcolonial Reading of *Dubliners,*" recasts that work as a covertly subversive narrative that both represents and undermines English colonialism and imperialism. Eugene O'Brien, in "The Return and Redefinition of the Repressed: The Construction of Female Identity in the Writings of James Joyce," analyzes the place of Ireland in postcolonial studies and the way that the inclusion of Ireland in the postcolonial field must reshape the paradigm that had been used in considering postcolonial approaches to African, Asian, or Latin American literatures. O'Brien develops this issue by studying the development of female subjectivity in *Dubliners.*

Noting the lack of postcolonial readings of the Ithaca chapter of *Ulysses,* Jon Hegglund, in "Hard Facts and Fluid Spaces: 'Ithaca' and the Imperial Archive," reads the chapter as a parodic subversion of the structure of the "imperial archive." This term, which Hegglund borrows from Thomas Richards, "was the imaginative representation of an ideal repository of knowledge through which heterogenous data about the empire could be ordered and systematized" (Hegglund, chapter 3). Trevor Williams, in his essay "Mr. Leopold Bloom, Staunch Britisher: The Problem of Identity Under Colonialism," expands from the scene of Bloom questioned by the Watch in the Circe chapter of *Ulysses* to the general issue of identity (national, cultural, religious, linguistic, and so on) for anyone "brought up in the shadow of imperialism." William C. Mottolese's contribution to this collection, "Traveling *Ulysses*: Reading in the Track of Bloom," attempts to foreground the ways that late Victorian travel discourse shapes *Ulysses* significantly and in ways quite different from the mythic and epic versions of travel that had been treated in Joyce studies prior to postcolonial approaches.

Michael Tratner, in "What's Wrong with Hybridity: The Impotence of Postmodern Political Ideals in *Ulysses* and *Midnight's Children*" examines the dilemmas of hybridity in the postcolonial subject (against the "monologistic desire" of either nationalism or Marxism in relation to the colonial influence or the ruling class), as represented in these two key works by Joyce and Salman Rushdie, from different generations and places within the British Empire. Finally, Christy Burns, in her essay "Postcolonial Cartographies: The Nature of Place in Joyce's *Finnegans Wake* and in Friel's *Translations,*" offers a reading of conflicting cartographies of postmodernism and imperialism, arguing that the way language and cartography is treated by Joyce in *Finnegans Wake* "redefines Irish postcolonialism, moving it away from nationalist-homeland concerns and toward a diasporic position." She sets this view of *Finnegans Wake* against Brian Friel's 1981 play, which has become a touchstone in Irish postcolonial literary studies.

1

Topography and Transformation

A Postcolonial Reading of *Dubliners*

ALLAN H. SIMMONS

IN A LETTER TO CONSTANTINE P. CURRAN of 1904, Joyce described his intention in *Dubliners* (1914) as "to betray the soul of that hemiplegia or paralysis which many consider a city."[1] The origins of the collection lie in a request from George Russell (Æ), asking Joyce to write something "simple, rural?, livemaking? pathos? [pathetic]"[2] for the *Irish Homestead,* Joyce submitted "The Sisters," followed by "Eveline" and "After the Race."[3] Together, these three stories, published in the *Irish Homestead* in 1904 under the pseudonym "Stephen Dædalus," represent the only stories of the fifteen that comprise *Dubliners* to have been published serially. (The *Irish Homestead* rejected Joyce's fourth story, "Clay," the following year—possibly incurring the "fictional" Stephen's denunciation of it as "the pigs' paper" in *Ulysses* [*U,* 158]). Writing to William Heinemann, on September 23, 1905, Joyce described the volume as "an attempt to represent certain aspects of the life of one of the European capitals" (*Letters* 2, 109). Heinemann rejected the manuscript, which lead Joyce to offer it to Grant Richards, offering as his raison d'être:

1. In Gilbert 1957, 1:55. Henceforth, references to *Letters of James Joyce* will be abbreviated *Letters* followed by the volume number.

2. Letter at Yale. Cited in Ellmann 1983, 163.

3. "The Sisters," *Irish Homestead* 10, no. 33 (Aug. 13, 1904): 676–77; "Eveline," *Irish Homestead* 10, no. 37 (Sept. 10, 1904): 761; "After the Race," *Irish Homestead* 10, no. 51 (Dec. 17, 1904): 1038–39.

"I do not think that any writer has yet presented Dublin to the world. It has been a capital of Europe for thousands of years, it is supposed to be the second city of the British Empire and is nearly three times as big as Venice. Moreover, the expression 'Dubliner' seems to me to have some meaning and I doubt whether the same can be said for such words as 'Londoner' and Parisian' both of which have been used by writers as titles"(*Letters* 2, 122). Joyce concludes the letter: "I think people might be willing to pay for the special odour of corruption which, I hope, floats over my stories"(*Letters* 2, 123).

In October 1904, Joyce left Ireland with Nora Barnacle, and spent the next two and a half years in Pola, Trieste, and Rome. It was while living in Trieste, in 1905, that most of the stories in *Dubliners* were written. As an Italian-speaking enclave of the Austro-Hungarian Empire, Trieste afforded Joyce with not only a critical distance from which to examine Ireland but also a parallel political reality to Dublin: the Act of Union in 1801 incorporated Ireland into the United Kingdom of Great Britain and Ireland—a state of dependency and subordination that lasted until 1921. In this manner, the sense of detachment that is the stylistic hallmark of the collection enacts Joyce's own exile from Ireland. In "Ireland, Island of Saints and Sages," a lecture delivered on April 27, 1907, at the Università Popolare in Trieste, Joyce identified "the English despoiler" as "almost entirely a materialistic civilization," but he cautioned, too: "It is well past time for Ireland to have done once and for all with failure. If she is truly capable of reviving, let her awake, or let her cover up her head and lie down decently in her grave forever" (Joyce 1959, 173–74). Bounded by these imperatives, *Dubliners* thus depicts the economic, political, and cultural stasis of a colonized nation together with her struggles, often implicit and only dimly emergent, to contest and subvert imposed authority.

Joyce famously described his style in *Dubliners* as one of "scrupulous meanness" (*Letters* 2, 134), thus reflecting the overdetermined and circumscribed lives of its characters within the narrative act that constitutes them: the expression of Dublin life is inscribed in the very writing that recreates it. Rituals of containment structure the stories, and these, together with the persistence of themes such as alienation and isolation, suggest both paralysis consequent upon subjugation and the persistent resentment of this. In other words, Joyce's stories can be viewed in terms of subtle but significant unease. His Dublin is not the Dublin of grand subversive gesture but rather of persistent individual disquiet, suggesting that the colonized cannot and will not submit wholly to definition of them as subject. As the stories frame and elaborate each other, in a nested structure, everyday events are invested with the solidity of national mythology, and it is in this light that the reader comes to recognize the range of postcolonial counterstrategies to colonialism they employ to reflect resistance to England as, simultaneously, futile and yet enduring.

Any attempt to address a text from a postcolonial perspective must necessarily recognize that this perspective is a reaction to a logically prior "colonial" perspective with which postcolonialism is in revisionist dialogue.[4] In turn, this has implications for the status of the text: is it an authentic reflection of a historical moment, or a critique of this moment? This essay will thus consider *Dubliners* as a portrait of English colonialism in Ireland within which is contained a subversive covert narrative in which this hegemony is undermined.

Joyce identified the structural unity of *Dubliners* in terms of personal maturation: "stories of my childhood . . . stories of adolescence . . . stories of mature life . . . [and] stories of public life in Dublin" (*Letters* 2, 111). But any implication of progression is immediately offset as the opening story announces the keynote to the collection, "paralysis," and connects this to other themes that will characterize the volume. Even before the young narrator's fascination with "the word *paralysis*" (*D*, 7) is explicitly stated, in the first paragraph of the story, it is implicitly present in the subject and condition of the opening sentences:

> There was no hope for him this time: it was the third stroke. Night after night I had passed the house (it was vacation time) and studied the lighted square of window: and night after night I had found it lighted in the same way, faintly and evenly. If he was dead, I thought, I would see the reflection of candles on the darkened blind for I knew that two candles must be set at the head of a corpse. (*D*, 7)

4. As Lloyd argues: "The 'post' in post-colonial refers not to the passing of colonialism but to the vantage point of critiques which are aimed at freeing up the processes of decolonialization from the inhibiting effects of nationalism invested in the state form" (1999, 41).

The proclaimed hopelessness is stylistically reinforced in the monosyllables with which the tale begins—significantly, the first polysyllable, "vacation," occurs in parenthesis—and in the use of repetition. That this is focalized through a child, already familiar with the religious rituals of death, thematically announces the stasis of Dublin life. The fact that "paralysis" exerts a fascination comparable to "the word *gnomon* in the Euclid and the word *simony* in the Catechism" (*D*, 7) in the narrator's mind extends its influence, by association. If the inhibiting influence of religion is expected—"I do not see what good it does to fulminate against the English tyranny while the Roman tyranny occupies the palace of the soul" (Joyce 1959, 173)—the geometric image is more subtly prefigurative. A gnomon is a parallelogram from which a smaller, similar parallelogram, containing one of its corners, has been removed. The figure thus represents both incompleteness and correspondence: incompleteness, obviously, because its shape is defined by an absence, the missing parallelogram; and correspondence, because the parallel lines structurally connote the comparable lives of the Dubliners and, more pertinently, the parallel cultures of host and visitor in colonized Ireland. Parallel lines are equidistant, and therefore, by definition, they neither diverge nor converge. This has implications for Joyce's representation of the relationship between Ireland and Britain: their nondivergence reflects (colonial) mimicry and their nonconvergence (postcolonial) resistance.

The absent parallelogram in the gnomon defines a shape by lack: our early appreciation of geometric form means that we "read" the gnomon by the "something missing." Of course, in postcolonial terms, this spatial absence equates to Ireland. Not only is this how Ireland is perceived by its conquerors and betrayers, and one may well argue that the absence defines and is subsumed by the shape, but this is a further contested site: Ireland's absence resists inclusion and fragments the symmetry of the parallelogram on whose form the identity of the gnomon depends. The colonial construction of identity "functions first of all through a Manichaean logic of exclusion" (Hardt and Negri 2000, 124). According to Fanon: "The colonial world is a world cut in two" (1963, 38). The shape of the gnomon alerts the reader to the importance of boundaries.

Fittingly it is the preservation of boundaries that is the sine qua non of colonialism, distinguishing between "us" and "them." But these same boundaries provide the locus for the play of differences that is realized in hybridity and resistance. Thus, what we might think of as the shape of colonialism works against itself to subvert the power of its ruling structures.

It is not going too far to argue that Joyce is instructing the reader how to read *Dubliners* in "The Sisters." First, the young narrator's fascination with words emphasizes language as a semiotic system, within which words like "gnomon" have precise reference and history. The child's-eye view generates a gap between comprehension and incomprehension that the reader is encouraged to fill: interpretation occupies the place of authority vacated by Father Flynn and, by extension, the church. Although Old Cotter's unfinished sentences offer a linguistic counterpoint to the finished life of Father Flynn, their incompleteness conforms to a pattern: the boy cannot remember the end of his dream; similarly, Eliza's gesture—"She laid a finger against her nose and frowned" (*D*, 16)—indicates that she does not want to say any more in front of the boy. But this pattern, in turn, recalls the (similarly incomplete) gnomon. Joyce's concern with stasis as represented by determined form and boundaries in *Dubliners* gains from the inclusion of another geometric shape, the quincunx, in "Grace," originally the final story in the collection. Such symmetry, reinforced by similarities between the two tales that bookend the collection (religion as a shared theme; Father Flynn's paralysis echoed in Father Purdon "struggling up the pulpit" [*D*, 196]; the place of candles in each), naturally suggests another defining form: the circle.

Throughout the volume, circularity is used to portray stasis and the entrapment of Dublin life. The stories of "childhood"—"The Sisters," "An Encounter," and "Araby"—reflect a childhood world of thwarted intentions and frustrated endeavor. Mimetically recounted through the (egocentric) use of first-person narration, they pose the question of how Dubliners can escape the "nets" identified by Stephen Dedalus in his conversation with Davin in *A Portrait of the Artist as a Young Man* (1916): "When the soul of a man is born in this country there are nets flung at it to hold it back from flight. You talk to me of nationality, language, religion. I shall try to fly by those nets" (*P*, 207).[5] In the tales that follow flight or progress is presented

5. Stephen's words summarize what Joyce said during a public lecture in Trieste in 1907: "The economic and intellectual conditions that prevail in [Ireland] do not permit

as impossible: the circumscribed lives of the characters, often mirrored in their literal journeys, are characterized by circularity.

The circularity present in the early tales—say, in the repeated phrases by the "josser" in "An Encounter" or the analepsis in "Eveline" that returns the narrative to "the odour of dusty cretonne" (*D,* 37, 41)—is variously developed in the later tales: Lenehan's peregrinations in "Two Gallants" while waiting for Corley to return lead him back to where he started; in "Counterparts" Mr. Alleyne's bullying of Farrington is structurally repeated in his bullying of Tom; when Maria sings "I Dreamt that I Dwelt," in "Clay," she repeats the first verse instead of progressing to the second, and, in the same story, young Alphy Donnelly shares his name with his uncle, while the description of Maria's nose almost touching her chin is repeated three times; the cyclical nature of life is recorded in such anniversaries as Ivy Day, Halloween (in "Clay"), and Christmas (in "The Dead").[6] In addition, intertextuality lends an air of stasis to the collection as a whole—through such parallels as the missing corkscrew (in "Clay" and "Ivy Day in the Committee Room") and the reappearance of characters from one tale in another. Thus, in "Grace," the congregation at Gardiner Street Church (where the Dillons also attend mass in "An Encounter") includes Mr. Fanning, Father Keon's business associate in "Ivy Day in the Committee Room," and the reporter of *The Freeman's Journal,* Mr. Hendrick, from "A Mother."

But this circularity does more than confer a sense of stasis upon Joyce's representation of Dublin life. It is intimately associated with the issue of colonialism, as can be seen in Gabriel's anecdote about his grandfather's horse, Johnny, in "The Dead":

---

the development of individuality. The soul of the country is weakened by centuries of useless struggle and broken treaties, and individual initiative is paralysed by the influence and admonitions of the church, while its body is manacled by the police, the tax office, and the garrison. No one who has any self-respect stays in Ireland, but flees afar as though from a country that has undergone the visitation of an angered Jove" (1959, 171).

6. Here and elsewhere, when arguing for the cyclical nature of Irish history, I am working toward a different end to that envisaged by McClintock when she writes: "The term 'post-colonial' . . . is haunted by the very figure of linear development that it sets out to dismantle" (1992, 85).

> Out from the mansion of his forefathers . . . he drove with Johnny. And everything went on beautifully until Johnny came in sight of King Billy's statue: and whether he fell in love with the horse King Billy sits on or whether he thought he was back in the mill, anyhow he began to walk round the statue. . . . Round and round he went. (237–38)

However comically, Johnny's reaction to the statue of William III of Orange, whose defeat of James II at the Battle of the Boyne in 1690 helped bring about the Protestant Ascendancy in Ireland, reflects both enthrallment and fascination, attitudes that underscore the attitude of the Dubliners to the English in the stories. First and foremost, then, the statue is consistent with the iconography of oppression. As Jackson and McGinley remind us: "Irish Nationalists celebrated the horse for throwing the supremacist king to his death" (1995, 185f; the king's horse stumbled over a molehill). The reference to the statue within "The Dead" is thematically complemented by Bartell D'Arcy's song "The Lass of Aughrim," as William III defeated an army of Irish and French soldiers here in 1691. The statue, which has since been removed, stood in College Green at the heart of Dublin. Offering a concrete reminder of conquest that is nonetheless capable of being reduced to ridicule in a family tale, simultaneously an expression of colonial domination and a site of postcolonial resistance, the statue demonstrates the manner in which stories in *Dubliners* identify and trace fault lines between what we might identify as the ruling and subaltern classes, while resisting the temptation to stray into historical revisionism. Put another way, the very symbols that extend the collection's sense of paralysis to colonial stagnation reveal fault lines, suggesting that the colonially imposed social hierarchy itself is porous. It should be noted that while the memory of Johnny (and it is surely significant here that, like Michael Furey, it is a *memory*), circling the statue of William III, reinforces Joyce's concern with determined form and boundaries in *Dubliners*, it also identifies a key strategy in colonial subjugation: "consensual subservience," in Cheng's felicitous phrase (1995, 109).

Reminders of British colonial presence in Dublin are everywhere in the collection. Overtly, the concrete expressions of domination include the Wellington Monument, the Castle, and the soldiers embarking at the North Wall at the end of "Eveline." (The Allan Line ships conveyed British soldiers, stationed in Irish garrisons, between Dublin's North Wall harbor and

Liverpool—whence the Allan Line also sailed to Canada, calling at Buenos Aires.) Similarly, in its oriental resonance, the "Araby" bazaar underscores the extent of the British Empire, a point reinforced when the disenchanted narrator remarks on the "English accents" (35) at the tale's conclusion.[7] Invariably noted at moments of humiliation in the stories, the English accent is intimately associated with feelings of subjugation. Thus, just before he fails "to uphold the national honour" (106) in a test of strength against (the presumably English) Weathers, Farrington—whose sensitivity to intonation originates, in part at least, from Mr. Alleyne's "piercing North of Ireland accent" (95)—hears the woman he has been ogling say "*O, pardon!* in a London accent" (106), as she brushes against his chair. Although frustrated, Farrington's desire for the English woman is itself a colonial platitude: the assumed desire of the colonized for the colonizer. But, more pervasively, the English presence in these two stories is synonymous with financial exploitation. Weathers not only defeats Farrington in the test of strength, he also drains his finances, all the while "protesting that the hospitality was too Irish" (104).

The colonial adage, "trade follows the flag," is, of course, an inversion of the truth since, as the authors of *The Oxford History of Britain* point out: "In almost every case, it was the opposite" (Matthew and Morgan 1992, 42). The tales in *Dubliners* demonstrate the degree to which economic suppression is a chief weapon in the colonizer's armory. When Maria goes shopping in "Clay," she clutches her purse emblazoned with the words: *"A Present from Belfast"* (111). Together with the fact that Maria, a Catholic, works for Protestants at the *Dublin by Lamplight* laundry, and her literal status as a poor old woman, one of the "names given her [Ireland] in old times" (*U*, 12), her purse functions as a signifier of Protestant England's economic stranglehold over Catholic Ireland, here seen to be symbolically controlling

7. The Conroys' goloshes—"Guttapercha things" (*D*, 205), from Malay *getah percha*, "gum-tree"—in "The Dead" provide another connotator of Empire. Joyce himself visited the Araby bazaar when it visited Dublin in May 1894 (Ellmann 1983, 40). A further oriental association can be traced in the name, Mangan. This possibly derives from the Irish poet James Clarence Mangan, of whom Joyce claimed (in 1902): "Eastern tales . . . have rapt him out of his time" and "East and West meet in his personality" (Joyce 1959, 77,78).

the very purse strings.[8] From this angle, a poignant myopia affects Maria's self-image: "She arranged in her mind all she was going to do and thought how much better it was to be independent and have your own money" (113). Of course, instances of financial impoverishment are widespread in the tales. One thinks, for instance, of the bleak inventory of Mr. Duffy's uncarpeted room in "A Painful Case" (119), of Lenehan's dinner in "Two Gallants"—"a plate of hot grocer's peas, seasoned with pepper and vinegar" (61–62)—or of the streets through which the narrator in "Araby" carries his "chalice" of devotion for Mangan's sister, "jostled by drunken men and bargaining women, the curses of laborers, the shrill litanies of shop-boys who stood on guard by the barrels of pigs' cheeks, the nasal chanting of street-singers, who sang a *come-all-you* about O'Donovan Rossa, or a ballad about the troubles in our native land" (31). It is clearly not just Joyce's style but the lives of the Dubliners he portrays that can be described in terms of "scrupulous meanness" (*Letters* 2, 134). Such examples reinforce the unifying central theme of paralysis, representing national impoverishment in material terms. But where a connection can be drawn between financial impoverishment and imperialism, it makes sense to interpret such poverty as political, serving to support and sustain British hegemony over the Irish.

Politics and economics overlap in "After the Race," whose very title, through the use of the word "race," invites the reader to examine its latent imperial content. Although the themes of speed and movement offer a counterpoint to the paralysis found elsewhere in the collection, the images of automobile and yacht ultimately serve to reinforce the stasis of Dublin life by contrast: the racing cars and drivers are foreign, and the yacht aboard which the tale concludes is owned by the American, Farley. The theme of colonial subjugation, together with the quiescence of the Irish in their subjugation, is identified at the outset:

> The cars came scudding in towards Dublin, running evenly like pellets in the groove of the Naas Road. At the crest of the hill at Inshicore sightseers

8. It is surely no coincidence that during the divination game, in which Maria picks clay (representing death), the alternatives mentioned—the prayer-book (her second chance, suggesting a religious life), the ring (marriage), and water (travel)—do not include, as is traditional, money.

> had gathered in clumps to watch the cars careering homeward and through this channel of poverty and inaction the Continent sped its wealth and industry. Now and again clumps of people raised the cheer of the gratefully oppressed. (44)

The juxtaposition between national "poverty and inaction" and foreign speed, wealth, and industry is stark, while the (repeated) identification of the Irish, as "clumps" of people, enacts the familiar reductive colonial trope of viewing the colonized collectively rather than individually. Topography extends hegemony still further as, to enter Dublin, the Naas Road must pass between potent symbols of British occupation: Richmond Barracks and Kilmainham Gaol. In this context, the description of the Irish as consensual—they are "the gratefully oppressed," actively celebrating the foreigner's victory—identifies the basis upon which hegemony depends while adumbrating the theme of economic oppression to follow. Mr. Doyle, Jimmy's father, "who had begun life as an advanced Nationalist," but "had modified his views early," confirms the degree to which Ireland is complicit in her own servitude.[9] "A butcher in the significantly named 'Kingstown,'" he has "been fortunate enough to secure some of the police contracts" (45) and, thus, actively nourishes the oppressor. Furthermore, it is his money that will help to fund Ségouin's motor business in France. It is surely no accident that, when Ségouin and Rivière drop off Jimmy and Villona, to prepare themselves for dinner at Ségouin's hotel, it is near the Bank of Ireland (itself the Irish Parliament until 1800). The hotel—like Farley's yacht, to which they subsequently journey—provides a further image of the transient nature, and hence the superficiality, of the visitor's concern for the host culture.

Besides financing Ségouin's enterprise, the Doyles' "Irish money" (47) will also be gambled away in the all-night card game, in which "Farley and Jimmy were the heaviest losers" (51). Although the yacht provides the only instance in *Dubliners* when the action strays offshore (into Kingstown Harbour), any suggestion of escape proves illusory: not only is mobility the province of foreigners in this tale, but, as if to confirm that political suppression

9. As Cheng notes: "Jimmy Doyle's English education reflects how shoneen values get inculcated in subaltern groups through processes of social formation and education" (1995, 106).

manifests itself in economic terms, it is the Englishman, Routh, who is the eventual winner at cards.[10] Jimmy's opinion of his companions only confirms his place in the ranks of the "gratefully oppressed": "What jovial fellows! What good company they were!" (50).

Correspondingly, resistance itself is portrayed as futile: although Jimmy succeeds in rousing "the torpid Routh" when voicing "the buried zeal of his father" (49), the city into which the men emerge shortly afterward wears "the *mask* of a capital" (49; my emphasis).

Nor is Jimmy Doyle the only character in *Dubliners* who is portrayed as raising the cheer of "the gratefully oppressed"—which he does quite literally when joining in the toasts to Ireland, England, France, Hungary, and the United States of America. Deference to and mimicry of the oppressor are presented in various forms. In "A Little Cloud," Ignatius Gallaher returns to "the old country" (81) on a visit from London. His visit awakens Little Chandler's sense of the parochialism of Dublin: "if you wanted to succeed you had to go away. You could do nothing in Dublin" (79). This sentiment, that voices the paralysis at the heart of the collection, gains from Gallaher's colonial and patronizing comments about "dear dirty Dublin" (82) and "old jog-along Dublin" (85). The mere prospect of meeting his erstwhile friend again awakens Little Chandler's discontent with his lot. Focalized through him, the narrative contains hints of Little Chandler's own poetic style, which he imagines as *"A wistful sadness . . . The Celtic note"* (80), that point up its incongruity with the prosaic reality of "poor stunted houses" (79) and the "vermin-like life" of "grimy children" (77). By contrast, Corless's (whose name subversively suggests an absent "core"), where the two men meet, offers Little Chandler (another name pregnant with reductive associations) a glimpse of a privileged, cosmopolitan world, where people "eat oysters and drink liqueurs" served by waiters who "spoke French and German" (78). While Chandler seems out of place, having "trouble . . . catching the barman's eye" (83), Gallaher is at ease in this environment, as shown when he addresses the bar-staff familiarly as *"garçon"* and *"François"* (81, 85). The use of foreign phrases,

10. In "Two Gallants," Lenehan, whose circular journey I have already mentioned, wears a "yachting cap" (*D,* 52) while Corley's exploited "slavey" wears a "white sailor hat" (58). In each case, these connotators of escape function instead as derisory reminders of entrapment.

such as *"parole d'honneur"* (87), identifies language itself as colonial trope. In what amounts to colonial mimicry, Gallaher has adopted the speech habits of his adopted country, as can be seen in such turns of phrase as: "Thanks awfully, old chap" (87). Similarly, when he does uses Irish, *"deoc an doruis"* (87; a "drink of the door," or "one for the road"), he gets it wrong: *"deoc"* should be *"deoch."* As in "After the Race," it is not simply the English who are perceived as oppressors. Gallaher's assertion that Parisians have "a great feeling for the Irish" (84) gains when one remembers that the nations share a religion (Catholicism) and a common enemy (England). Overtly, this seems to distinguish between continental and English values—and it is noticeable that it is Gallaher's story about an *English* duchess that "astonished" Little Chandler (85)—but his anecdotes about sexual morality abroad that prove so unsettling to the Chandler marriage are drawn from Paris and Berlin as well as London. That the Irish Gallaher should articulate their cumulative disruptive force illustrates the degree to which the colonized, paradoxically, reinforce and enact the processes of colonization in these tales.

As has been widely noted, "Two Gallants" offers a codification of Irish entrapment. For instance, noting that the "solid sound of his boots had something of the conqueror in them" (59) as Corley approaches the young woman, Jackson and McGinley detect a colonial paradigm analogous to John Bull's treatment of Kathleen ní Houlihan: "He violates her then he takes her money" (1995, 49f). The presence of the harpist in the story reinforces this interpretation: the description of his harp as "heedless that her coverings had fallen about her knees" and "weary alike of the eyes of strangers and of her master's hands" (58) extends this symbol of Ireland to the young woman herself.[11] This interpretation of the story as an allegory of colonial exploitation is

11. The intimacy of this image has been anticipated in "Araby," where the young narrator confesses: "My body was like a harp and her words and gestures were like fingers running upon the wires" (31). A further point to note here concerns the description of Corley's "conquest" in "Two Gallants": She remains "a young woman" until she furnishes him with the gold coin, when she becomes merely "A woman" (64). A variant on this theme of lost identity is provided in "Counterparts" where Farrington's employers address him by his surname; his first name, Tim, is then provided by "the boys" for whom he is buying drinks in the Scotch House bar (104); and, his humiliation complete, at the end of the evening he is simply "A very sullen-faced man" (107).

complicated by the presentation of the Irish collusion. In terms that anticipate Stephen's description of Buck Mulligan in *Ulysses*, Lenehan calls Corley "Base betrayer!" (56) But, since Lenehan himself profits from Corley's "deep energetic gallantries" (62), he too is complicit in the exploitation and thus extends the betrayal-theme. Corley and Lenehan thus represent the subaltern culture, mimicking the practices of the oppressor. In his letter to Stanislaus Joyce of September 25, 1906, Joyce described the story "with the Sunday crowds and the harp in Kildare Street and Lenehan" as portraying "an Irish landscape" (*Letters* 2, 166). Betrayal is a characteristic feature of this "landscape": Corley is "the son of an inspector of police" and is "often to be seen walking with policemen in plain clothes, talking earnestly" (54–55). The implication is that Corley is an informer for Dublin Castle, the literal and symbolic presence of English domination in Ireland. Among the ranks of the shoneen in *Dubliners* are to be found Mr. Moony—"a sheriff's man" (66)—in "The Boarding House," and Jimmy Doyle's father, in "After the Race."[12] Most obviously, "Ivy Day in the Committee Room" delineates how hegemonic consent operates, through such references to "shoneens that are always hat in hand before any fellow with a handle to his name" (135) and "Castle hacks" (140), supported by recurrent insinuations about the collaborative role of the church in ousting Parnell from power, and the jibe aimed at Major Sirr: as the head of the Dublin police, Major Henry Charles Sirr (1764–1841) was reliant upon Irish informers.

Thus far, the image of Ireland that I have responded to in *Dubliners* has largely been one of colonial hegemony, supported by the "gratefully oppressed." However, as Joyce said: "When a victorious country tyrannizes over another, it cannot logically be considered wrong for that other to rebel" (1959, 163). Thus, in various and subtle ways, the collection also resists this reading and poses a postcolonial reaction to it, and it is to the reactionary tropes that I now wish to turn. Traditionally and, it must be said, romantically, Ireland is perceived as rustic. Of course, it suited England's

12. Doyle's father's early "advanced Nationalist" views identify him as a Parnellite and supporter of Home Rule and Parnell. However he has "modified" these. He is based upon William Field (1848–1935), who the *United Irishman*, edited by Arthur Griffiths, described as a "flunkey" of the crown (see Jackson and McGinley, 35 and 41).

purpose politically to maintain a rural Ireland: within an imperial dialectic, this perception enables the binary distinction between town and country, between modernity and primitivism. As his decision to make his quintessential Dubliner in *Ulysses* a Hungarian Jew demonstrates, Joyce has a vision of Ireland that breaks the rules. The Ireland of *Dubliners* is urbanized, metropolitan, and Anglicized, and Dublin a site where cultures come into contact and modify each other. His focus throughout is the middle and lower-middle classes, rather than, say, the slum dwellers, at one extreme, or the politically and economically powerful, at the other. The question for us is whether these moribund and drink-sodden lives merely confirm a pantomimic and colonial representation of the Irish or whether they are capable of resisting such racist constructions. The long line of drunks in the tales culminates in Freddy Malins in "The Dead."[13] Asked by Aunt Kate to control him, Gabriel is thus thrust into the role of enforcer. Allegorically, the cosmopolitan Gabriel occupies the position of the Castle to Freddy Malins's Ireland. Various aspects of Freddy's character identify him with images of Ireland developed across in the collection. For instance, in his ability to converse with Lily he reveals a depth of feeling that will be associated with Irishness in this story and which will counterpoint Gabriel's own emotional paralysis. Significantly, he also repays money to Gabriel in the story, but, unlike the economic enthralment addressed in, say, "After the Race," this transaction has an air of honor about it, leading Gabriel to confirm him as "a decent sort of chap," albeit in a "false voice" (248). The fact that *Dubliners* is largely concerned with the very class to which Freddy belongs lends an important note of postcolonial resistance to his challenge to the Protestant and aptly named Mr. Browne: "And why couldn't he have a voice too? Is it because he's only a black?" (227).

As my examples of mimicry have demonstrated, Joyce is attentive to the inauthenticity of the Dublin word, to which Father Purdon's sermon and Gabriel's after-dinner speech contribute. But in this context, too, Freddy's is an important countervoice. When Aunt Julia sings "Arrayed for the Bridal," "Her voice, strong and clear in tone, attacked with great spirit the runs which embellish the air and though she sang very rapidly she did not miss

13. See Lloyd (in Attridge and Howes 2000) for a discussion of Joyce's use of drink "as an element of unincorporated cultural difference" (138).

even the smallest of grace notes. To follow the voice, without looking at the singer's face, was to feel and share the excitement of swift and secure flight" (220). The general applause, to which Gabriel contributes "loudly," is inauthentic: "It sounded so genuine that a little colour struggled into Aunt Julia's face" (220). The way that Freddy responds, however, is very different. The description of Freddy, "with his head perched sideways to hear her better" (220), suggests a deeper engagement with the song's narrative: he has felt and shared its proffered "excitement of swift and secure flight." While his prolonged applause and cumbersome compliments may strike a sentimental and slightly inauthentic note—Aunt Julia's old voice has clearly sounded better—Freddy's response is not derided by Joyce and offers, perhaps, the most objective affirmation of authenticity in the story. The fact that this is the affirmation of a sentimental drunkard illustrates how "The Dead" reasserts positive qualities without becoming romantic.

Joyce's proposed follow-up volume to *Dubliners,* to be entitled "Provincials,"[14] did not materialize. In the absence of the *rus* versus *urbs* comparison that this volume may have afforded, country Ireland is derided. For instance, in "The Dead," Gretta is sneeringly referred to as "country cute" (213) by Gabriel's mother, and although rural Ireland is invoked through references to the Aran Isles (215) and Gretta's nostalgic desire—"I'd love to see Galway again" (218)—this is offset by the tale's theme of thwarted longing coupled with Gabriel's detachment from his "own land" (216). In "A Mother," Miss Kearney's name is deliberately chosen: not only is Kathleen is an allegorical name for Ireland (one thinks of Lady Morgan's song, "Kate Kearney"), but the blatant associations with "Kate Kearney's Cottage" in County Kerry—to which her "Irish picture postcards" (154) and study of Gaelic lend support—suggest an alternative rural vision of Irishness to set against urban Dublin. However, the cultural paralysis in the tale (offering a variant on the political paralysis found, say, in "Ivy Day in the Committee Room") is undermined by her repeated submission to her overbearing mother.[15]

14. See letter to Stanislaus Joyce, July 12 , 1905; *Letters* 2, 92.

15. In *Ulysses,* Molly Bloom refers derisorily to "Kathleen Kearney and her lot of squealers Miss This Miss That Miss Theother lot of sparrowfarts skitting around talking about politics they know as much about as my backside" (*U,* 627). There is also the suggestion that

Similarly, in "Grace," provincial Ireland is at once depicted as backward and instrumental in colonialism. Thus, the constable has a "suspicious provincial accent" (170), while Martin Cunningham's humorous depiction of the police force involves mimicking "a thick provincial accent" (181). The police are also referred to as "ignorant bostooms . . . thundering big country fellows, omadhauns" (181), from the Irish, *bastún,* meaning bounder, and *amadán,* meaning fool. For his part, Jack Power is "employed in the Royal Irish Constabulary Office in Dublin Castle" (173). The Royal Irish Constabulary was the police force for Ireland outside Dublin. As Jackson and McGinley note, "It ran an armed intelligence force, charged with maintaining British hegemony over Ireland through the use of spies" (1995, 138k). But it would be a mistake to suggest that rural Ireland merely replicates the condition of colonial paralysis offered by Dublin, for, as the example of "The Dead" proves, the countryside is also associated with latent, untamed—and possibly untameable—forces that overwhelm the metropolitan and international Gabriel. In this light at least, Joyce's failure to produce the "Provincials" volume, albeit by serendipity, retains the possibility of a postcolonial reaction and revision through "absent" forces as yet unnamed and, consequently, untamed.

Topographically, the Dublin setting for the stories contains obvious colonial elements. Chief among these, references to Dublin Castle in the tales function as shorthand for English colonial presence. In other words, its presence is simultaneously mimetic and symbolic. But, in *Dubliners,* such sites also provide opportunities for subversion. For instance, the description of Martin Cunningham in "Grace" as being "a Castle official only during office hours" (181) simultaneously identifies his collusive role in the hegemony and implies that this is merely a role—a point underscored by the fact that the description occurs as a prelude to his joke at the expense of the police force. At one level, which we might think of as colonial, topography introduces

---

Hoppy Holohan's name may be a mocking variant on "Kathleen ni Houlinhan." Given the feminist claim that colonialism is a hypermasculine construct, it is worth noting that the identification of Kathleen with Ireland in "A Mother" links colonialism and gender. According to Mrs. Kearney: "They wouldn't have dared to have treated her like that if she had been a man. But she would see that he daughter got her rights" (*D,* 167).

parallels between London and Dublin: for example, there are references to Mansion House, Fleet Street, and Temple Bar ("A Mother," 163; "Counterparts," 112). While extending the idea of mimicry and asserting the colonial attempt to subsume the colonized into its governing frame of reference, such shared names serve also to stress the parochialism of Dublin by comparison with London. But attention to topography in the collection reveals a covert, often ideologically subversive narrative, which we might describe as postcolonial. As Lloyd has argued pertinently: "In the discrepancy between the spatial and temporal logics of the colonial state, or the new nation-state, and the recalcitrant practices they must contain emerges a novel and unstable interface at which social formations are continually reconstituted" (1999, 46). Joyce's scrupulous attention to the layout of Dublin attracts attention and invites deeper consideration. To take a trivial example: the fact that Mrs. Mooney moves from Spring Gardens to Hardwicke Street in "The Boarding House" seems of little consequence in itself. But once contextualized—The Marriage Act (1754) of Philip Yorke, Earl of Hardwicke, abolished Fleet marriages—the detail is seen to have a direct bearing on story. In this light, the fact that Father Flynn dies in "Great Britain Street" without fulfilling his desire to revisit "Irishtown" carries allegorical, if obvious, meaning.[16]

Of course, realist fiction tends to be located in real geographical settings, but, as Joyce demonstrates in *Dubliners,* this context contributes a narrative of its own. Indeed, as Joyce presents it, Dublin contains so many architectural and nomenclatural reminders of colonial domination that it is difficult not to read locale as an expression of colonial (and postcolonial). During their day's "miching" (20) in "An Encounter," the boys cross the River Liffey. On their way to the north bank they pass the site of the Battle of Clontarf, site of an Irish victory over the Danes in 1014; once on the south bank, where the eponymous "encounter" occurs, they are near the landing place of invaders from the Vikings to Oliver Cromwell (in 1649).[17] In other words, the topog-

16. The fact that Great Britain Street has been renamed Parnell Street is itself symptomatic of postcolonial revisionism.

17. Readers will be aware that in this section I draw on the assiduous research of Jackson and McGinley (1995) whose annotated *Dubliners* is an essential tool for scholars interested in this novel.

raphy of the story, with its connotations of invasion and resistance, provides a historical and political context for personal experience. Once we attend to details of this order, it becomes clear that Joyce's mimetic use of locale simultaneously asserts the brute fact of colonialism (this is colonized space) and offers the potential for transformation through awareness of the historical context. That this contextual inscription is the responsibility of the reader renders the act of interpretation itself postcolonial and subversive.

In *Dubliners* Joyce proves that the details of narrative setting are never simply contingent or innocent. Instead, the topographical circumstances have interpretive consequences beyond their mimetic function. For example, knowing that Father Purdon, S.J., "a man of the world like ourselves" (186), shares his name with Purdon Street in Dublin's notorious "Nighttown" complicates the presentation of Catholicism in "Grace": Should we read this association as ironically equating religious salvation with Nighttown, or, contradictorily, transcendent, for, while Father Purdon may be thus identified with Nightown, he remains unaffected by it—in which case, is he really "like ourselves"? Similarly, the fact that Corley's assignation with the young woman in "Two Gallants" takes place at Donnybrook, site of the famous fair, lends to the encounter associations of the "carnivalesque." But, read in this light, the encounter troubles the reading I have offered above as it is spatiotemporally associated with a period of misrule rather than the norm. More typically, topography can be seen to serve a political purpose in the tales. When Farrington walks home in "Counterparts" it is "in the shadow of the wall of the barracks" (107–8). This reminder that Dublin is an occupied city associates Farrington's personal sense of entrapment with the prevailing colonial hegemony. More subtly, In "A Mother," where cultural commitment to the Eire Abu Society is offset by avarice, Mrs. Kearney's self-serving is politicized when we learn that the family holiday in seaside resorts with large Protestant populations: "If it was not Skerries it was Howth or Greystones" (154).

The emotional paralysis of "A Painful Case" gains when one learns that Chapelizod, a former garrison village, where James Duffy lives, derives its name from the Celtic princess, Izod (Isolde) and is thus underscored by Wagner's romantic opera of frustrated love. While Chapelizod is a suburb of "the city of which he was a citizen" (119) in the tale, Jackson and McGinley point out that, at the time of the story, it was "distinct from Dublin, three miles further down the Liffey" (1995, 95c). In view of Joyce's topographical accuracy elsewhere in the collection, it is tempting to read this instance of spatial flexibility as destabilizing: it may well relocate the garrison within the city precincts but, even as it does so, this redrawing of the map threatens the very shape and locus of colonialism established elsewhere in the collection.[18]

Nowhere is the postcolonial function of Joyce's use of topography more acutely expressed than in its historical dimension. As the places mentioned in *Dubliners* bear the historical imprint of previous colonization, so these historical definitions locate their present incarnation in the time of the narrative present within the broader truth of historical change. Furthermore, historicizing reminds us that cultures are inevitably partial and hybrid formations and thus always in an important sense resistant to colonialism. The physical presence (and historical endurance) of Dublin within the stories is utilitarian (in the sense that, as setting, "every part of it has a function in the action" (Prince 1987, 87). It is, among other things, connotator of mimesis, colonial garrison, and "mask of a capital" (*D*, 49). But, more importantly, the city's presence reminds us that English colonialism, too, shall pass. But if, as Stephen Dedalus famously says, history is "a nightmare" (*U*, 28), the awakening retains unsettling memories. Historicizing the topography of *Dubliners* allows us to see thematically consistent forces, such as betrayal, in the grain of the past. Baggot Street, where the "slavey" in "Two Gallants" is employed, was formerly, Gallows Road, where the Parliamentarians defeated the Royalists in 1649, paving the way for Cromwell's invasion of Ireland. The Wicklow Street setting for the committee room in "Ivy Day in the Committee Room" offers a point of intersection between oppression

18. Coincidentally, Jackson and McGinley identify a report that appeared in *Freeman's Journal* on July 14, 1904 (1995, 99) as the source of the story of Mrs. Sinico's death. But Duffy only reads about the accident, in his (unionist) *Dublin Evening Mail,* in November (*D*, 124). Taken together, the examples thus subvert spatial and temporal order, and, by extension, carry the suggestion that prevailing systems of order, generally, can be changed. (Ellmann offers an alternative source for Mrs. Sinico's story [1983, 210n]). Although rebutted by Stanislaus, it none the less suggests that the accident was not unique.)

and resistance: the name "Wicklow" means "meadow of the Vikings," and Parnell was born in County Wicklow.[19] It is when we historicize topography in *Dubliners* that the volume's postcolonial dimension becomes most apparent. Spatially, colonialism attempts to encompass the totality of Dublin and, temporally, it presents itself not as a transitory, time-bound moment but rather as atemporal and permanent. The continuities and discontinuities between past and present that are inscribed in the geographical detail are thus indicative of the struggle to contest and subvert colonial definition. In other words, colonialism and postcolonialism contend in the topography of these tales—and the colonial present, brought to the bar of history, is found wanting.

Setting off for his meeting with Gallaher in Corless's, Little Chandler passes under "the feudal arch of the King's Inns" and "deftly" makes his way "through all that minute vermin-like life and under the shadow of the gaunt spectral mansions in which the old nobility of Dublin had roistered" (77). Here, as elsewhere in the collection, connotators of oppression and entrapment coexist with assurances about the movement of history. In this sense, the past is, paradoxically, both paralyzing and liberating. Geographically determined space, complimented by references to geometrical form, encourages a (colonial) reading of Irish life as static. But this interpretation does not allow for the representation of boundaries as porous and fluid in the collection that gains from the historicizing of topography and locates *Dubliners* at a point of intersection between past and present, between colonial entrapment and postcolonial resistance. This encourages attention to form elsewhere in the collection, with which I shall conclude this essay.

The cultural backdrop to *Dubliners* is provided by the resurgent interest in Irish tradition in the late nineteenth and early twentieth centuries. The writings of W. B. Yeats, Lady Augusta Gregory, and J. M. Synge, for instance, mine the rich vein of ancient sagas. The Gaelic League provides a measure of

19. Unsurprisingly, it is the memory of Parnell himself in this story that synthesizes its postcolonial forces. For instance, the implied analogy between Parnell and Edward VII—and thus between Kitty O'Shea and the king's alleged mistress—both elevates Parnell to the status of king and reduces difference, the "otherness" on which colonialism depends, to an essential similarity.

the popular appeal of this expression of national identity: founded in 1893, it had nearly six hundred branches by 1908. The timing of the Irish Revival is significant: it responds to the vacuum created in constitutional politics by the death of Parnell (in 1891) and to the disabling leadership-struggle in revolutionary politics. In "A Mother," however, Joyce extends the depiction of paralysis in the collection to include the Irish trapped between imitation of the English and the moribund nature of Irish Revival culture that Irish nationalism took up in the 1890s. Nor does the marketing of the movement escape Joyce's attention. One imagines that images such as the "Irish picture postcards" (154) exchanged between the Kearney sisters and their friends lie behind Jackson and McGinley's claim: "To Joyce the kitsch of the Irish Revival was as bad as—or worse than—the flummery of the British Empire" (1995, 134). Nonetheless, a deeper engagement with Irishness lies behind Miss Ivors's question to Gabriel Conroy: "And why do you go to France or Belgium . . . instead of visiting your own land?" (215). By contrast with the Kearneys—and, of course, Gabriel himself—Miss Ivors holidays in the traditionalist West of Ireland. This suggests an ongoing cultural dialogue between the different stories in the collection. As the cultural counterpart to the Home Rule movement, the Irish Revival sought, in particular, to resuscitate the use of Gaelic: "And haven't you your own language to keep in touch with—Irish?" (215). While the decline of the language in the nineteenth century can be attributed to a range of factors, including emigration and the Great Famine,[20] the chief cause was the gaining perception of English as the language of power, commerce, modernity, and internationalism.

The power of colonialism depends upon orienting the colonized in terms of the colonizer's semiotics. In this sense, language is indicative of colonialism creates the world it inhabits. As Hardt and Negri argue, "The colonized's mimicry of the colonizer's discourse rearticulates the whole notion of identity and alienates it from essence" (2000, 144). The loss of linguistic identity is, therefore, instrumental in the loss of social, cultural, and political identity. Written in English, *Dubliners* reflects the historical fact

20. Although referred to as the Great Famine, it was, in fact, a series of famines from 1845 to 1850, during which 1.1 million Irish people died of starvation. (See Wilson 2002, 74–83.)

of colonialism.[21] Furthermore, as we have seen, the collection advertises its concern with language on the opening page. Taken together, these two facts invite ideological consideration: does appropriation coexist with subversion?

Linguistically, what we might term "Dublin English" is conveyed, like topography, for purposes of realism. The stories resonate with instances of slang—"I was too hairy to tell her that" (54)—and idiom: "wanted for to go" (17). While such idiomatic expressions clearly breach "standard" English they, none the less, confirm hybridity—a point Mrs. Kearney fails to realize when responding patronizingly to accent and idiom in "A Mother," where language itself is politicized. Mr. Duggan's "yous" have not prevented him from appearing in "grand opera" (160), whereas her emphasis upon *artistes,* graphologically indicated in the text, is further derided with each repetition. In a tale about the Irish Revival, Mrs. Kearney's obsession with accent as a social marker—"And who is the *Cometty,* pray?" (158)—is unequivocally colonial. Stressing her hypocritical allegiance to the movement, at times her mimicry is deconstructive, as when she haughtily upbraids Mr. Holohan: "You must speak to the secretary. It's not my business. I'm a great fellow fol-the-diddle-I-do" (168). This echoes the ballad, "Whack Fol the Diddle," written by Peadar Kearney, who also composed the Irish national anthem.

Although such misuse of the English language as Eliza's malapropism "rheumatic [instead of "pneumatic"] wheel" (16) in the opening story is humorously reductive (although, unconsciously, her adjective extends paralysis to the forces of modernity here), as Mr. Henchy demonstrates in "Ivy Day in the Committee Room" such linguistic playfulness, used consciously, can be subversive. Imagining himself as a City Father "in all my vermin" (143), Henchy's pun punctures the pomposity of the ermined political aristocracy. In fact, the transformation of "ermine" into "vermin" does more than simply subvert authority: Since the unity of the collection means that one reads the tales as being in dialogue with each other, the pun echoes the "vermin-like life" (77) through which Little Chandler passes. Through this association, the pun serves to blame the "ermine" for the Dublin slums, then

21. It is worth noting here Joyce's cosmopolitan vision: "What race, or what language . . . can boast of being pure today? And no race has less right to utter such a boast than the race now living in Ireland" (1959, 165–66).

among the worst in Europe. According to Kiberd, their mortality rate was higher than Calcutta's at the time (1996, 219).

But the issue of language in the stories extends to the instance of Gaelic words, which is concentrated in the last stories in the collection. Up to this point, as we have seen, the language inheres in place names that engage with the forces of history by revealing, palimpsestically, earlier stages in the place's identity. As the process of colonialism involves reorienting the Other in terms of the colonizer's semiotics, the fact that stories are presented in English suggests the silencing and eradication of the native, Gaelic tongue. That Gaelic becomes a feature of *Dubliners* from "Ivy Day in the Committee Room" onward suggests that it cannot be eradicated. Tracing this broad structural pattern reveals language as a further site for postcolonial resistance. Functioning mimetically, Irish expostulations pepper "Ivy Day in the Committee Room," which contains the highest incidence of Irish words: for example, the narrative includes "Musha" (136), meaning "indeed," and its variants "Usha" (137, 139) and "Wisha" (143), together with "shoneens" (135), "moya" (138), and, "Yerra" (142). Most obviously the repeated use of Gaelic expressions here underscores the story's theme of political ineffectuality: like the *"Pok!"* with which the bottles of stout are uncorked, the words reduce to hot air. This further serves as a critical reminder of Irishness betrayed in the treatment of Parnell. Nevertheless, the very presence of Gaelic in this story of political canvassing affirms the place of language as a site of contestation. This is then developed thematically in the following story, "A Mother," where the Eire Abu Society offers a blend of Irish cultural heritage and nationalism. But, rather than provide a means of resisting the colonizer, language here dramatizes the petty conflicts that handicap the cultural revival and, by extension, political resistance. For instance, pronunciation provides the focus for Mrs. Kearney's self-serving and social snobbery. A locus for divisions among the colonized, language is robbed of its potential to challenge the colonizer. Read as reflecting the author's own feelings, the suggestion is that Joyce has flown by Eire Abu, flown by Stephen's "nets," and that he cannot be co-opted easily into the celebratory elements of the Irish revival.

Providing a more complex use of Gaelic is "Grace," with which, in Joyce's original conception, *Dubliners* was to have concluded. Words such as "bostooms" and "omadhauns" are used to denigrate "country bumpkins" (181) who now serve as policemen for the Castle. Language is thus used ambivalently: as a means of postcolonial subversion, denigrating the authorities, it implicitly confirms the shared linguistic heritage of the colonized; but Gaelic is identified with rural Ireland, and the colonial representatives are Irish "bumpkins," so turning language upon them is deconstructive, suggesting that Ireland's is a culture threatening to unravel itself. In this manner, colonial authority is challenged *and* maintained simultaneously. Joyce's attention to language in "The Sisters" calls attention to its development across *Dubliners,* in particular to the incidence of Dublin or Irish colloquialisms and the further evolution of this into Gaelic. That said, to have ended the collection there would have promoted, at best, a qualified postcolonial presentation of language; Joyce's decision to add "The Dead" reasserts the claims of Irish culture, structurally ensuring that this is the collection's destination, and this is effected largely through the story's susceptibility to the revivifying claims of language.

"The Dead," and hence the volume, ends with Gabriel's epiphany. This is simultaneously Gabriel's personal epiphany and a linguistic epiphany. Across the collection, the scrupulous meanness of Joyce's style has functioned as an analogy for the state of mind of the inhabitants of Dublin, revealing their humdrum lives in prose that is itself humdrum. The very epiphanies to which characters such as Little Chandler are led serve only to illuminate the entrapment and stasis of their colonized, urban predicaments. In Joyce's hands, the epiphany—from the Greek word for "manifestation" (and obviously freighted with Biblical echoes)—typically employs a trivial incident, such as Little Chandler's meeting with Gallaher, in order to crystallize and so illuminate an aspect of the paralysis that is the condition of Dublin life for those who people these tales. By contrast, Gabriel's epiphany, which is ultimately linked to his ability to recognize the authenticity of the love between Gretta and Michael Furey, is reinforced by the poetic quality of the language in which it is couched and which, fittingly, mimics his revelation. Indeed, had Gabriel's epiphany merely revealed to him his own failure to love Gretta with the passion associated with Michael Furey—and thus to the state of his marriage—it would be consistent with other epiphanies in *Dubliners,* dramatizing the paucity and restrictedness of his own life. Instead, as Gabriel's meditations demonstrate, this epiphany has prolongations into broader, national, and cultural themes and exploits the poetic potential of language. In so doing, it breaks free from the thematic and linguistic stasis of the rest of the collection in order to reassert the claims of Gaelic culture in a gesture that, when seen in terms of the narrative arc of *Dubliners,* describes a postcolonial celebration of Irishness.

To take one example, when Mr. Alleyne uses chiasmus to threaten to Farrington, the figure is stylistically analogous to the repetitive circularity of Dublin life as portrayed: "You'll apologize to me for your impertinence or you'll quit this office instanter! You'll quit this, I'm telling you, or you'll apologize to me!" (101). The structural reversal is faintly subversive, seeming to turn Mr. Alleyne's threat back upon himself. The same rhetorical figure is employed in the final sentence of *Dubliners*: "His soul swooned slowly as he heard the snow falling faintly through the universe and faintly falling, like the descent of their last end, upon all the living and the dead" (256). Together, free indirect discourse and chiasmus unite Gabriel's "swoon" with the snow falling outside—and, by extension, with the world beyond his hotel window, with the countryside stretching westward beyond Dublin, and with the "lonely churchyard on the hill where Michael Furey lay buried" (256), a world whose presence is evoked onomatopoeically through the combination of assonance, alliteration, and sibilance. Here chiasmus describes not so much entrapment as Gabriel's reconnection with his own Irishness. This identification with his cultural roots, embodied in the wife he has seen as if for the first time, is a crucial development in the narrative of *Dubliners.*

Structurally, "The Dead" divides into two sections: the Misses Morkan's annual dance and Gabriel's epiphany, which begins with the leave-taking. As elsewhere in the collection, and, perhaps, reflecting the weight of the past upon the present, the epiphany is shorter than the preceding narrative section (from which, as in another love story, "Eveline," it is separated typographically). Seen through a postcolonial lens, this pattern is ambiguous: while suggesting that Ireland is held back by her traditions, it creates through a form of suspense and expectation a mounting desire for release into the present that, obviously, involves a release from colonial domination. But there is more to it: the image of the past that storms Gabriel's thoughts in the final pages is no longer associated with paralysis. He is left with the quiet yet tragic acceptance of a truth about his relationship with Gretta: he can never fulfill her in the manner that Michael Furey did. He recognizes that, in many senses, he is a lesser figure than Michael Furey. Yet knowing this makes him a more substantial figure than the Gabriel who worried about his after-dinner audience's possible response to the Browning references in his speech. Unlike previous epiphanies that belittle the subject, Gabriel's does not diminish him, despite his sense of longing and the knowledge that he will never possess Gretta. The conclusion of the story offers no solution to either this harsh truth or the Irish condition. Gabriel recognizes that "the time had come for him to set out on his journey westward" (255). The fact that the story ends without him embarking on this journey retains the sense of stasis that typifies Dublin life elsewhere in the collection. Henceforth, he may well make forays to the west of Ireland, but these will doubtless alternate with his holidays abroad. The political conditions of life will not change: the "journey westward" links the twin inferences of death and Ireland. Instead, the suggestion that Gabriel now has the capacity to begin such a journey authenticates him—while leaving the political and cultural complexity that cannot simply be unpicked by looking westward, even though this, too, is now a necessary part of his existence.

Articulating the two halves of "The Dead," and the occasion for Gretta's recollections, is the song "The Lass of Aughrim." On one reading, this is a song about the feudal lord's droit du seigneur and the consequent exclusion of the Irish peasant woman, the "lass" of the song's title, from her position in society because she has cohabited with the aristocratic Lord Gregory. Conflating colonialism and sexism, it thus implicitly and allegorically recalls the reality of English imperialism—through which associations it looks back to "Two Gallants" and forward to Gabriel himself. But Gabriel, representative of continental values in the story, who holidays abroad "partly to keep in touch with the languages and partly for a change" (215) and for whom "Irish is not my language" (216), will come to see the limitations of colonial attractions and steer his thoughts homeward. Linked to the volume's concern with the authenticity of the Irish voice is the question of whose is the appropriate singing voice for this song, that of Mr. Bartell D'Arcy or Michael Furey. Names loom large in our interpretation of "The Dead": for instance, given the context of Irish Catholicism, the names of the two men in Gretta's affections, Gabriel and Michael, inevitably recall the two archangels, juxtaposing and conferring their qualities, guardian and militant. Both in terms of nomenclature and setting the two singers are distinguished: the aristocratic and English-sounding Mr. Bartell D'Arcy sings to a select audience indoors, excusing himself "roughly" on the grounds that he's "as hoarse as a crow" (241); Michael Furey, whose very name resonates with the passion, sang the same song in the rain and as an expression of authentic affection, rather than as a concert piece.[22]

In Bartell D'Arcy's rendition, "The song seemed to be in the old Irish tonality and the singer seemed uncertain both of his words and his voice" (240). The repeated use of the modalizing locution, "seemed," suggests that, in Mr. Bartell D'Arcy, Joyce is portraying the appropriation of Irish traditions by the English who nonetheless miss their true value. Seeing Gretta enraptured by the song, Gabriel envisages her as the subject of a painting entitled *Distant Music* (240). Although Gabriel cannot know it at this point, the image extends to Michael Furey and to the tradition of Irish art. The suggestion is that while the English, here represented by D'Arcy and Gabriel, beautify and aestheticize such art, they rob it of its subversive power, founded upon a shared heritage that gives voice to culturally definitive suffering. Not so for Gretta: she responds to the reality of Michael Furey—and, ultimately, as his epiphany demonstrates, Gabriel goes as far as it is possible for a husband to go by accepting this.

Viewed in terms of the collection as a whole, "The Lass of Aughrim" completes the process whereby national aesthetics—toward which Joyce's volume contributes in no small measure—functions postcolonially: as an escape from paralysis. Reflecting Joyce's own artistic interests, musical references punctuate the stories. Of particular significance are those to the opera *The Bohemian Girl* (1843), by the Dublin composer Michael Balfe (1808–70). Together with *Maritana,* by William Wallace, and *The Lily of Killarney,* by Sir Julius Benedict, Balfe's *The Bohemian Girl* constituted what

22. In his essay "Gaelic Folk Songs" (1890), Douglas Hyde, founder and president of the Gaelic League, argued of Irish folk songs that "though in their origin and diffusion they are purely local, yet in their essence they are wholly national, and, perhaps, more redolent of the race and soil than any of the real *literary* productions of the last few centuries" (1986, 107).

was called "the Irish Ring." Mr. Duggan, in "A Mother," has sung the part of the king in *Maritana* (16),[23] and Frank has taken Eveline to see *The Bohemian Girl* (40), from which Maria's song, "I Dreamt that I Dwelt" (118) is drawn, in "Clay." These references underscore the longing for escape that is heard in the various references to Bohemia as an ideal every bit as pertinent as the Aran Isles mentioned in "The Dead." Jimmy Doyle pronounces the merriment aboard Farley's yacht in "After the Race" as "Bohemian" (50) while Ignatius Gallaher finds Dublin parochial after "all the Bohemian cafés" of Paris (83). But it is not until "The Dead" that such connotations of escape and freedom function as anything more than ironic reminders of entrapment. As I have argued, "The Lass of Aughrim" signals a change in direction, offering at the level of aesthetics a solution that depends upon the intimate relationship between a nation and its culture.

That Michael Furey should have worked in the distinctly unromantic Galway gasworks subtly links the urban and rural settings, suggesting the pervasive and transformative potential of Irish culture in this story. Whereas in, say, "A Mother," the narrative attitude toward Gaelic traditions is derisive, in "The Dead" this becomes increasingly more nuanced. For example, how should we treat Molly Ivors—as an interfering busybody, as a naïve romantic, or as a true patriot? The increasing claims of a specifically Irish past in the story suggest the latter. That she should unsettle and pose a puzzle for Gabriel suggests the reassertion of old, as opposed to contemporary Ireland, embodied in the feeling and essentialism of Michael Furey. Extending the place of Gaelic in the collection, her valedictory *"Beannacht libh"* (223)—literally "blessing to you" (i.e., goodbye)—has more authenticity in a tale where the recurrent references to the west signify both Ireland and death. Transforming the earlier nationalism-as-death theme, through Gretta and Michael Furey, the west is associated with love, too. It is this revitalizing potential that has been missing from the earlier stories. Structurally, this is what has been missing from the gnomon-shape that has defined *Dubliners* and, fittingly, "The Dead" was inspired by Joyce's sense that his depiction of

23. In the same story, we learn that Mr. Bell, the second tenor, competes each year at the "Feis Ceoil" (160), established in 1897 as part of the Irish Revival and in which Joyce competed as a solo tenor, in May 1904, winning the bronze medal.

Irish life in *Dubliners* was incomplete, like the figure of the gnomon itself. Conjoining the West of Ireland and Dublin, "The Dead" finally binds "the living and the dead" (256) in a manner that articulates national tradition and the international, modern world. It is possible to interpret the use of "The Lass of Aughrim" in the story as atavistic and romantic, but this would be to overlook comparison with Hynes's song in "Ivy Day in the Committee Room" and thus the developmental shape of *Dubliners* as a whole. Ironically framed and subject to platitudinous appreciation, "The Death of Parnell" serves only to suggest that Parnell was finer than the system that brought him down and thus to confirm the paralyzing force of that gnomonic system. Put another way, the absence that defines the parallelogram as a gnomon has not been replaced and Joyce's scepticism about his countrymen is epitomized in the myopia of Mr. Crofton's final comment—on the style of Hynes's poem and not its message. By contrast, "The Lass of Aughrim" finds a way to replace the absence, by reaffirming the authenticity of Irishness, while yet retaining the exile's clear-eyed view of home. To have reached this conclusion is the collection's ultimate achievement.

2

The Return and Redefinition of the Repressed

The Construction of Female Identity in the Writings of James Joyce

EUGENE O'BRIEN

THAT POSTCOLONIAL STUDIES has become a seminal part of academic life is now beyond debate. Indeed, the very term "postcolonial" has become the latest "catchall term" to "dazzle the academic mind" (Jacoby 1995, 30) by becoming part of the "intellectual/academic industry taking as its topic the colonial division of the world" (Smyth 1995, 27). At an epistemological level, however, there has been considerable debate as to the epistemological status of postcolonialism:

> Such has been the elasticity of the concept *postcolonial* that in recent years some commentators have begun to express anxiety that there may be a danger of it imploding as an analytic concept with any real cutting edge. (Moore-Gilbert 1997, 11)

A further level of complexity is introduced into this debate when the matter of Ireland is considered. Luke Gibbons has speculated that the problem with Ireland and postcolonial studies is simply that "a native population which happened to be white was an affront to the very idea of 'white man's burden,' and threw into disarray some of the constitutive categories of colonial discourse" (Gibbons 1996, 149). However, academic opinion has diverged considerably on this issue.[1]

1. A thorough discussion of the usage of this term in a specifically Irish context is to be found in Attridge and Howes 2000, 1–21.

There has been ongoing debate about this topic within the academy, with some theorists, notably Bill Ashcroft, Gareth Griffiths, and Helen Tiffin, in *The Empire Writes Back: Theory and Practice in Post-Colonial Literatures* (1989) and in *The Post-Colonial Studies Reader* (1995), arguing that Ireland was complicit in the colonizing of other cultures and hence cannot be seen as part of the postcolonial paradigm. The point here is that the complicity of Irish soldiers in the "British colonial enterprise" makes the Irish seem more colonizer than colonized and makes it difficult for "colonized peoples outside Britain to accept their identity as post-colonial" (Ashcroft, Griffiths, and Tiffin 1989, 33). Liam Kennedy makes a similar point, suggesting that "Ireland, in effect, was a junior partner in that vast exploitative enterprise known as the British Empire" (1996, 176). Declan Kiberd, however, demurs from this position, noting that *"The Empire Writes Back,* passes over the Irish case very swiftly, perhaps because the authors find these white Europeans too strange an instance to justify their sustained attention" (1996, 5). Kiberd's point is well taken, and Caitríona Moloney and Helen Thompson have made the relevant suggestion that in order for Ireland to be considered "part of the postcolonial paradigm, the paradigm itself must change" (2000, 4). Perhaps this is the key to the point at issue. There can be no doubting the value of postcolonial theory as an instrument of critique. Colin Graham makes the valid point that

> it is these abilities to read culture as ideological, while criticising the homogeneity of ideology, and to prioritise cultural interchange within a colonial structure, which makes postcolonial theory an essential critical tool for understanding Irish culture. (2001, 93)

However, if postcolonial writing is not to leave itself open to a tu quoque charge of setting up its own, inverted Manichean allegory,[2] then the complications involved in the constitution of any form of hybridity or liminality

2. JanMohamed 1995. JanMohamed's thesis (referring to a third-century Persian cult that saw God and Satan as absolutely separate and locked in eternal conflict) is that colonial literature subverts "the traditional dialectic of self and Other" (18) and sets up a fetishized "nondialectical fixed opposition between the self and the native" (19). Colonization, as an ideology, power relationship, and discourse, endorses such a fixed binary opposition, with the colonized self being defined in contradistinction to the colonized "other," and thus JanMohamed's point is well taken.

must be taken into account. The matter of Ireland, especially the work of the canonical writers Yeats and Joyce, has profound implications for the epistemological status of the postcolonial paradigm. Although Yeats can be seen as a poet of empire, as a central part of the canon of English literature, he can also be seen as imperial subject, as demonstrated by Edward Said's suggestion that while Yeats has been almost completely assimilated into the canons of "modern English Literature" and "European high modernism, he can nevertheless be seen as belonging to the tradition of 'the colonial world ruled by European imperialism'" (Said 1990, 69).

Perhaps the most interesting conclusion that can be drawn from Said's argument is that there can really be no simple either/or choice underlying the postcolonial paradigm if that paradigm is to perform any sort of transformative critique of current and past colonial enterprises.[3] As Ania Loomba notes, the question is now being asked of postcolonial theory as to whether in "the process of exposing the ideological and historical functioning of such binaries, we are in danger of reproducing them" (Loomba 1998, 104). Instead of this either/or choice, what is needed is a more nuanced form of interaction between selfhood and alterity, between colonizer and colonized. This is a form of critique that has been advocated by Jacques Derrida, who, speaking about his early neologism, *différance,* notes that it is "neither *this* nor *that*; but rather this *and* that (e.g. the act of differing and of deferring) without being reducible to a dialectical logic either" (Derrida 1981, 161). In terms of an investigation of postcoloniality, one can look no further than Joyce to problematize the epistemological status of the postcolonial while enhancing the validity of postcoloniality as an informed mode of critique.

3. I think, given the examples cited, that this is a real danger for the postcolonial paradigm. "To allow oppositions to become reified is to attenuate the possibilities of influence, interaction, intersection and ultimately, transformation. It is also to predicate one's theoretical premises on the past as opposed to the future. If the colonizer/colonized opposition is seen as definitive within a culture, even though, as in Ireland, the initial acts of colonization occurred hundreds of years ago, then ipso facto, developments in the fields of politics, society and culture are limited by this reified definition of self and other. Issues of identity are ultimately settled by reference to this terminus a quo from which all such identificatory politics derives. Such a perspective narrows the theoretical scope of postcolonial discourse, and oversimplifies complex issues of interaction and influence" (O'Brien 2003, 138).

The focal point of this chapter will be Joyce's exploration of female subjectivity in some early stories in *Dubliners,* with a specific exploration of "Eveline." In a book whose structure has been the topic of much discussion, the role of the female characters has been surprisingly neglected.

Issues of structure in *Dubliners* have been much discussed but it is a discussion that is generally delimited by Joyce's own commentary. As early as 1905 Joyce had established a fourfold division of three stories each for *Dubliners.* This structure changed somewhat as the number of stories grew. In the first chronological division, childhood, there are three stories ("The Sisters," 1904; "An Encounter," 1905; "Araby," 1905). In the second, dealing with adolescence, there are four stories ("Eveline," 1904; "After the Race," 1904; "Two Gallants," 1905–6; "The Boarding House," 1905). The third group of stories, dealing with issues of maturity, also contains four stories ("A Little Cloud," 1906; "Counterparts," 1905; "Clay," 1905–6; "A Painful Case," 1905). The final group, dealing with public life, consists of "Ivy Day in the Committee Room," 1905; "A Mother," 1905; "Grace," 1905; "The Dead," 1906–7).

Although there is no doubting the coherence of this structural outline, there are, nevertheless, other possible structural schemata that can be adduced from this collection, and one of these must surely be the role of the development of female subjectivity throughout the book. There is little argument that in Molly Bloom, Joyce creates one of the most resonant interpretations of the voice of a woman in contemporary literature, but there has been comparatively little attention given to his earlier female characters. There has been comparatively none given to the development of female subjectivity in *Dubliners.*

In this chapter, I examine the characters of Eveline and, more briefly, that of Mangan's sister in "Araby." I discuss how Joyce is in the process of tracing how the experience of women within the *Lebenswelt* of colonial Dublin differed from that of men, and this should strike a chord with the postcolonial paradigm given its particularist stance and its reluctance to accept overarching totalizations.[4] The importance of language in the construction

4. One of the key generative texts of the postcolonial paradigm is Gayatri Chakravorty Spivak's much-anthologized essay "Can the Subaltern Speak?" (1985). Indeed, this essay has

of subjectivity is a concern shared by Joyce and one of his more influential critics, the French psychoanalytic theorist, Jacques Lacan.

For Lacan, subjectivity is centered on the interaction of the developing ego with what he terms the "other"; the identity of the human subject comes about through a number of interactions between the individual and two orders of meaning that he has termed the imaginary and the symbolic. Lacan suggests that self-recognition, or to put it more correctly, misrecognition *(méconnaissance),* is constitutive of the development of the human subject. In the mirror stage, Lacan postulates a child seeing its image in a mirror and becoming fixated on the image, which is both unified and coherent, as opposed to the child's own inchoate motor development. However, the image is also two-dimensional as opposed to three-dimensional. The fragmented infant identifies with, and desires to be like, an image of such wholeness, a process that Lacan sees as seminal to the imaginary order:

> Imaginary relations are thus two-person relations, where the self sees itself reflected in the other. This dual imaginary relation . . . although structurally necessary, is an ultimately stifling and unproductive relation. The dual relationship between mother and child is a dyad, trapping both participants within a mutually defining structure. Each strives to have the other, and ultimately, to *be* the other in a vertiginous spiral from one term or identity to the other. (Grosz 1990, 46–47)

But while images of wholeness give us an image of ourselves as distinct from the world, they never align with us perfectly. In Lacan's account of the development of the ego, human identity is seen as emerging from the crossing of a frontier, from what he terms the "imaginary order" (the dyadic world of mother and child), into that of the "symbolic order," which is concerned with symbolic systems, language being the main one (though both stages continue to coexist within the individual afterward):

---

given a name to a particular subgenre of postcolonialism, namely subaltern studies. However, what is interesting is that the full title of this essay is seldom seen, namely: "Can the Subaltern Speak?: Speculations on Widow Sacrifice." The original focus on this most essentialist silencing of a gendered subaltern has often been lost in the ongoing success of Spivak's argument.

> Language in the realm of the imaginary is understood in terms of some full relation between word and thing; a mysterious unity of sign and referent. In the symbolic, language is understood in terms of lack and absence—the sign finds its definition diacritically through the absent syntagmatic and paradigmatic chains it enters into. As speaking subjects we constantly oscillate between the symbolic and the imaginary—constantly imagining ourselves granting some full meaning to the words we speak, and constantly being surprised to find them determined by relations outside our control. (MacCabe 1985, 64–65)

It is clear from a reading of "Eveline" that there is a "deflection of the specular I into the social I" (Lacan 1977c, 5). In other words, human subjectivity comes into being through an ongoing process of reflection in the "desire of the other" (Lacan 1977, 5), and this process is very different for the women of *Dubliners*. For Lacan, desire is the prime agency of human subjective development, and it is always directed at some form of otherness. As he puts it, writing about "The function and field of speech and language in psychoanalysis": "man's *[sic]* desire finds its meaning in the desire of the other, not so much because the other holds the key to the object desired, as because the first object of desire is to be recognized by the other" (Lacan 1977d, 58). For Lacan, the very nature of desire means that it is always unfulfilled: "I always find my desire outside of me, because what I desire is always something that I lack, that is other to me" (Sarup 1992, 68–69). In the establishment of the ego, as we have seen, the desire for some form of identity is paramount. From infancy, we seek to be desired and loved by the Other, a term which, as Bracher notes, alters as we develop. Initially, at the beginning of life, this designation refers to the "mother, then both parents, later one's peers, and finally any number of bodies or figures of authority, including God, Society and nature" (Bracher 1993, 24). In many ways, it is the growth and development of our notion of the other that structures the type of identity that we develop, and language is the material dimension where such development can take place. This is true at both a conscious and an unconscious level, given Lacan's oft-quoted maxim that "what the psychoanalytic experience discovers in the unconscious is the whole structure of language" (Lacan 1977a, 147).

So what we find in the early stories of *Dubliners* is that the "other" in which the female subjects attempt to develop is far different for the men than for them—in Spivak's title, the subaltern may have been silenced by colonial repression, but it was the widow that was sacrificed. In other words, the experience of colonization was very different for women: they were the repressed by the repressed in many instances. However, it is interesting that Spivak, too, shares with Joyce and Lacan the notion that subjectivity is intrinsically connected with language. The voicing of any sense of subaltern selfhood is bound up with the subjectivity that is created through a reflection in the societal, colonial, and imperialist mirror; that language is the crucial component of issues relating to postcolonial identity is a Joycean truism; and of course, Lacanian theory would argue that language is the seminal component in the construction of all subjectivity: "man *[sic]* speaks therefore, but it is because the symbol has made him man" (Lacan 1989, 39). In Joyce's relationship with the postcolonial, language is the key point at issue, a point embodied in the title of the collection *Semicolonial Joyce* (Attridge and Howes 2000).

This title has been taken from a quotation in *Finnegans Wake*: "Gentes and laitymen, fullstoppers and semicolonials, hybreds and lubberds" (*FW*, 152:16–17), and in their introduction, Marjorie Howes and Derek Attridge discus the importance of the quote, probing the complexity of the different oppositions contained therein (Attridge and Howes 2000, 1–20). For our discussion, the most interesting points about this quotation are the focus on grammar as imperative in the construction of any sense of colonial or postcolonial identity: "The familiar distinction between full stops and semicolons" that also gestures toward the "opposition between permanent and temporary inhabitants of a country, or 'stoppers' and 'colonials'" (Attridge and Howes 2000, 1). The blurring of gender roles in "gentes and laitymen" is of further interest as it leads us to the consideration of the female in the postcolonial ambit in general and in Joyce's work in particular.

Consider the case of Eveline Hill, in her "little brown house" (*D*, 26), the eponymous heroine of the fourth story in *Dubliners.* Her subjectivity, in Lacanian terms, is defined in terms of her own personal and social other, and it becomes clear that her position is far worse than that of her male family members. In a parallel of the Freudian repetition complex, her life, by the end of the story, will be seen to repeat many of the destructive patterns of her mother's before her. Her sense of self is predicated on a reflection in the men of her life at present, and in reflected memories of her past in terms of women and children. In terms of the mirror stage, her desire to be of some worth is located through the male gaze, whether that of her brother, her father, or her "fellow," Frank. Speaking of the moment at which the mirror stage comes to an end, Lacan says: "It is this moment that decisively tips the whole of human knowledge into mediatization through the desire of the other" (1989, 6). For Lacan, the notion of the other begins with an identification with an object different from itself, usually the mother, and then develops into the "Symbolic other, or the real father" (Ragland-Sullivan 1986, 16).

For Lacan, the initial object of desire is the identification with the image of the self in the mirror, a process symbolic of the identification with the "ideal-I." In Lacanian desire, there is an *objet petit a,* or an object that satiates need, which is already lost. For instance, the breast of the mother is lost to her child and never can be regained. The lost character of the *objet petit a* means that the subject can never regain the feeling of being whole. Thus, desire can never be satisfied by the object of its need, and its object is always elsewhere. The demand for love always exceeds the possibility of its satisfaction. In other words, the possibility of fulfilling desire through the procurement of a needed object falls away, and you are left with desire of the "other" in and of itself.

It is interesting that the role of the father is so important in this story, because for Lacan the development of subjectivity through language is predicated on what he terms the "Name-of-the-Father." In what is basically a linguistic reinterpretation of the Freudian Oedipus complex, he sees the metaphor of the "Name-of-the-Father" as substituting for the desire of the mother. In the initial mirror stage, the child, in the imaginary order, identifies with both its own ideal image and with the mother as the satisfier of all infantile demands. With the advent of entry into the symbolic order, the Name-of-the-Father substitutes for the presence of the mother, with the attendant sense of unfulfilled desire. In this story, however, the subject position of woman—both Eveline and her mother—is very much prescribed by their cultural context: they are both classic examples of lives that have been repressed at an almost systemic level.

For Eveline, her relationship with her mother has been foreclosed by death, and the sense of loss may be the reason for her perceived passivity.

This relationship has also been temporally frozen. Eveline's memories of her mother are specifically related to illness and death. The final hours of her mother's life repeat in Eveline's mind, specifically as she sits pondering her own decision. Here the repression of woman in this society becomes almost a pattern. The sound of the organ reminds her of the same sound at the time of her mother's death, and this in turn reminds her of the life her mother lead: "The pitiful vision of her mother's life laid its spell on the very quick of her being—that life of commonplace sacrifices closing in final craziness" (*D*, 29–30). The cause of that craziness has been hinted at earlier in the story, when evidence of her self-delusional logic is brought to the fore:

> She would not be treated as her mother had been. Even now, though she was over nineteen, she sometimes felt herself in danger of her father's violence. She knew it was that that had given her the Palpitations. When they were growing up he had never gone for her, like he used to go for Harry and Ernest, because she was a girl; but latterly he had begun to threaten her and say what he would do to her only for her dead mother's sake. (*D*, 27)

The subject position of Eveline's mother has become a fixed point from which Eveline's own subjectivity is delimited. Mrs. Hill's memory has become a Lacanian *point de capiton*,[5] a place where "signified and signifier are knotted together" (Lacan 1993, 268); her memory is frozen in her daughter's mind and her role as the reflective "other" for Eveline is similarly frozen and reified. Eveline's own subjective development is similarly atrophied by both the memory and by the final verbal injunction that fixes Eveline's position within the family. As her mother is dying, a relationship of imaginary fullness is created through Eveline's "promise to her mother, her promise to keep the home together as long as she could" (*D*, 29). This promise, made to a woman who was in the final stages of some form of dementia, has clearly attenuated Eveline's development as an individual. Her passivity and inability to communicate her feelings of angst to Frank in the final, voiceless

5. The term *point de capiton* has been variously translated in English as a "quilting point" or "anchoring point." In effect, it refers to moments in language that give the illusion of a fixed meaning; it is the point "by which the signifier stops the otherwise endless movement *(glissement)* of the signification" (Lacan 1977f, 303).

scenes at the North Wall create an eerie echo of her dying mother's inability to communicate with anyone, as she cried those much-analyzed words: "Derevaun Seraun! Derevaun Seraun!" (*D*, 30). The actual meaning of these words is immaterial—what is significant is the desire to communicate allied to an inability to communicate coherently. The parallel with Eveline herself is more to the point:

> Her distress awoke a nausea in her body and she kept moving her lips in silent fervent prayer. . . . No! No! No! It was impossible. Her hands clutched the iron in frenzy. Amid the seas she sent a cry of anguish. (*D*, 30)

In the circular logic of the story, she is seen sitting down in the opening lines, and rigid with fear, holding onto the iron railings of the North Wall, in the closing lines. This circularity is an index of her stunted development. Her "anguish" mirrors the "final craziness" of her mother and the incoherence of her clearly nonverbal cry is an echo of her mother's incoherent garbled final words. The combined imagery of stasis (the final image of the bedridden mother is important in this context) and of an inability to communicate is a clear indication of the repression of subjective development undergone by both women.

Eveline's choices are predicated on her male "others": her father and Frank. Both men are seen by Eveline as possessing an authority and an independence that far exceeds her own or that of her mother. Her father is first pictured striding through the field, brandishing his blackthorn stick, to bring the children home. His mastery over financial matters has already been discussed, and his sense of ownership of Eveline is also foregrounded in his dismissal of Frank's courtship and his interdiction against Eveline seeing him again.

Eveline's fear of her father is further underscored by the weekly row over money when, having handed her father her total week's wages (seven shillings) she had to endure a haranguing about thrift from her father before he would deign to return some of that money to her so she could shop for groceries. Clearly, Eveline is not highly prized by him, nor, given that this is her sense of selfhood, does she value herself highly. Frank is a different mirror image with whom she can identify. Interestingly, at first, Eveline is not interested in Frank qua Frank; rather is she interested in having a boyfriend:

"First of all it had been an excitement for her to have a fellow and then she had begun to like him" (*D,* 28). What we see here is the desire to be valued by the other. Her relationship with her father, despite her best efforts in attenuating his levels of violence, is based on fear.

Clearly, her father exercises a discourse of power over Eveline, a discourse that is paralleled by Frank's own. While never offering any threats to Eveline, Frank, too, encourages her passivity and sees her as a willing audience for his stories and adventures. They go to see *The Bohemian Girl,* and he sings to her, "about a lass that loves a sailor," calling her "Poppens out of fun," and, in a manner redolent of *Othello,* he "had tales of distant countries"(*D,* 30).

Once again, her role is passive; she listens, she accepts, and ultimately she is offered the choice of staying with her father (who she can only identify with by recalling an occasion when he dressed as a woman on a picnic) or stepping into the unknown with Frank, in Argentina.[6] Despite her work in the Stores, Eveline is pictured in the story as financially dependent, unlike the men in her life. Her father and Harry were able to achieve some form of financial freedom, and interestingly her father is seen twice in the story giving money: once in the weekly wrangle with Eveline, as he returns a portion of her wages to her, and second, in the memory of the last night of her mother's illness:

> She was again in the close, dark room at the other side of the hall and outside she heard a melancholy air of Italy. The organ-player had been ordered to go away and given sixpence. She remembered her father strutting back into the sick-room saying: "Damned Italians! coming over here!" (*D,* 29)

In terms of the power of money as an index of self-worth, her father and Frank, who bought the tickets for the boat, are both seen as authoritative and generous. Clearly their range of choices is larger than that of Eveline who can either keep house for her father in Dublin or for Frank in Buenos Aires.

Perhaps the most interesting incidence of her imaginary relationships that stunt her subjective development is the overweening presence in the story of

6. For an interesting discussion of the cultural and social aspects of emigration of women to Argentina, see Katherine Mullin's "Don't Cry for Me, Argentina: 'Eveline' and the Seductions of Emigration Propaganda" in Attridge and Howes 2000, 172–200.

the ultimate instrument of a repressive patriarchy, namely, the church. This is captured in a section of the story with masterly economy of style:

> And yet during all those years she had never found out the name of the priest whose yellowing photograph hung on the wall above the broken harmonium beside the coloured print of the promises made to Blessed Margaret Mary Alacoque. He had been a school friend of her father. Whenever he showed the photograph to a visitor her father used to pass it with a casual word: "He is in Melbourne now." (*D*, 27)

The fact that she is never initiated into this particular discourse of mastery even to the limited extent of knowing the name of the priest is interesting as it establishes a sense of the social other within which her subjectivity could develop as highly repressive. It is as if, repressed themselves by colonialization, the patriarchal agencies in Ireland ensure that their power base is not threatened by women. The other religious references, to the promises of Blessed Margaret Mary Alacoque, is also highly significant. She was a member of a visitation order of nuns in France in the seventeenth century. She was granted a number of visitations, and her poster would have contained a number of promises made by, supposedly, the sacred heart (a metonymy for Jesus) to those who displayed a picture of the sacred heart in their homes and who received the Eucharist on the first Friday of every month. Their function, in creating an attenuated societal other for women, is twofold. The first two promises stress the stratified and hierarchical structure of society that is being advocated: "I will give them all the graces necessary in their status in life" and "I will establish peace in their homes" (Gifford 1982, 49). The other important consideration is that woman here is merely a vehicle for the enunciation of the discourse of a male representation of divinity.

Thus, Eveline can see herself as a similar vehicle for both her father's strictures against Frank and Frank's stories and his plans for their putative life in Argentina. Marriage is the only sense of subjective fullness that Eveline can imagine: It will allow her to become the desire of the other because her social other will then have to acknowledge her personhood:

> But in her new home, in a distant unknown country, it would not be like that. Then she would be married—he, Eveline. People would treat her with respect then. She would not be treated as her mother had been. (*D*, 27)

The teleological status of marriage for woman in this context is clear, as is Eveline's capacity for self-delusion: her mother's marital status was the cause of, as opposed to the relief from, her mental and physical problems in her life.

For Joyce, the role of these women in a colonized culture is infinitely worse than that of men. It is as if they are a subspecies of colonized within a colonial setting. Given that imperialism and colonialism set out to ensure that all of the benefits of social, cultural, and economic activity returned from the colonies to the imperial center, there is an implicit allegorical connection between the actions of Eveline Hill and that of Ireland itself. In terms of choices, Eveline's life is governed by male parameters: she can choose to go with Frank or to stay with her father. In a broadly similar way, colonized societies found their choices delimited by the colonial structures within which they had to exist. As Loomba has said, even postcolonial critique, a very self-aware discourse, is often bound up in a Freudian repetition complex because it merely inverts the binary within which it had been previously marginalized.

In terms of economics, Eveline's being forced to give up her wages to her father who then returns a portion of them so that she can buy groceries for the house is another analogue of the colonial process. Countries in the third world were made dependent on goods produced by the imperial center. On being paid for their own raw material, they often find that the only desirable goods on which to spend it are manufactured by the imperial center, thus ensuring economic dependence and a viable and ongoing colony that does not need a huge repressive apparatus to ensure loyalty. Eveline's monetary situation is almost a paradigm of this type of economic dependency.

Similarly, in colonial ideology, the aim is very much to ensure that there is a created loyalty within the colony to the colonizing power. This is very much the tenor of Macauley's programmatic "Minute on Indian Education," which makes this point from the colonial perspective in its attempt to create a "class of persons, Indian in blood and colour, but English in taste, in opinions, in morals, and in intellect" (McCauley 1995, 430). Eveline, in her defense of her father, in her sense of identification with her home, and ultimately in her reluctance to embrace any form of transformative experience, embodies this process exactly. In this sense, she also embodies a repressed subclass within the postcolonial world of Joyce's Dublin; a class that is repressed by those who have been repressed themselves. Female subjectivity in these stories is created by identification with a male other whose sole aim is to dominate and repress it, a process that parallels that of the broader imperial and colonial project. As we have seen in "Eveline," this societal other is constructed in such a way as to delimit the opportunities for women to develop beyond certain clearly stratified limits.

The incipient stages of such a process are made clear in the story that just precedes "Eveline," namely, "Araby." In this story, the organizing trope is the classic quest motif, as the young narrator sets off to an exotically named destination to win a prize for the woman he loves. Of course, the story is a parody of the quest in the sense that the boy, instead of communicating with the object of his love, displaces his libido and instead sets off to get her a gift. The most interesting aspect of this story is the construction of the subjectivity of the beloved object (and this term is used advisedly). First, just as Eveline has the choice of belonging to her father or to Frank, so the girl in question here is nameless—except in terms of a male descriptor: she is referred to as "Mangan's sister" (*D*, 20). In this sense she is the *objet petit a* in Lacanian terms; she is the lost object that initiates the chain of desire within the narrator himself. For Lacan, the very nature of desire means that it is always unfulfilled: "I always find my desire outside of me, because what I desire is always something that I lack, that is other to me" (Sarup 1992, 68–69). However, desire itself is partially narcissistic, because the subject's desire for the other is also the desire for some reciprocation: "The first object of desire is to be recognized by the other" (Lacan 1989, 64). However, instead of seeing the girl as another subject, in her own right, her role in this story is merely as an object around which the narrator's own desire is channeled.

From the first mention of the girl, it is her effect on the narrator that is the major point detailed. She is seen as a body, as an other, and often different parts of the body act as metonyms for her totality:

> She was waiting for us, her *figure* defined by the light from the half-opened door. . . . Her *dress* swung as she moved her *body,* and the *soft rope of her hair* tossed from side to side. . . . While she spoke she turned a silver bracelet round and round her *wrist.* . . . The light from the lamp opposite our

> door caught the *white curve of her neck,* lit up her *hair* that rested there and, falling, lit up the hand upon the railing. At fell over one side of her dress and caught the *white border of a petticoat,* just visible as she stood at ease. (*D*, 20, 21, 22; my emphasis)

She is almost a set of different body parts, all of which elicit a sexual response from the narrator. She is very much the object of his scopic drive, and her function is to designate his developing subjectivity as one who is in love: "the Other is, therefore, the locus in which is constituted the I who speaks to him who hears" (Lacan 1977e, 141). She is not so much another subject as an *objet petit a,* a signifier of the boy's desire and of his societal development from a boy to a young man. In this sense, women in *Dubliners* often fulfill this function—one thinks of the narrator in "An Encounter" where, having spoken of his friends' enjoyment of literature of the Wild West, he tells of liking "better some American detective stories which were traversed from time to time by unkempt fierce and beautiful girls" (*D*, 9).

In this story, the almost disembodied figure of Mangan's sister serves the same effect, functioning as an image from which the boy's development can be traced. She is always the object and never the subject in this story. Like colonized countries, to whom the *Pax Romana* or the *Pax Britannica* is brought, whether they want it or not, Mangan's sister is valued for her role in defining the narrator and for nothing else. She functions as an image for him of his own maturity: "Her image accompanied me even in places the most hostile to romance" (*D*, 20). Her role is to embody this image of desire—she has no other value than this. Just as Frank came home from Argentina looking for a wife, and found her in Eveline, so the narrator of this story is looking for some form of object of desire through which his own sense of selfhood can be reflected, and Mangan's sister, with he disembodied existence in his mind, can provide this object. It is worth noting the number of possessive deictics in the following passage:

> *I* imagined that *I* bore *my* chalice safely through a throng of foes. Her name sprang to *my* lips at moments in strange prayers and praises which *I* myself did not understand. My eyes were often full of tears (*I* could not tell why) and at times a flood from *my* heart seemed to pour itself out into *my* bosom. *I* thought little of the future. *I* did not know whether *I* would ever speak to her or not or, if *I* spoke to her, how *I* could tell her of *my* confused

> adoration. But *my* body was like a harp and her words and gestures were like fingers running upon the wires. (*D*, 21; my emphasis)

Her role is to reflect back to him an enhanced image of himself: through the scopic drive, the power of the gaze. It is her image as opposed to her sense of selfhood that is the object of his desire. The image of her as a chalice, to be borne by him through the crowd, is an interesting index of possession of an inanimate object that is ripe for filling with his own desire. Similarly, even the sound of the rain falling conjures up images of her, with obvious phallic undertones in the image of the "fine incessant needles of water playing in the sodden beds" (*D*, 21). She is the image that allows him to see himself as a young man in love: "I pressed the palms of my hands together until they trembled, murmuring: 'O love! O love!' many times" (*D*, 21).

Hence, his journey to the exotically named bazaar Araby is a journey undertaken through the eye of the other: he imagines that he is being looked at by her as he travels across Dublin to bring her a gift: "The syllables of the word Araby were called to me through the silence in which my soul luxuriated and cast an Eastern enchantment over me" (*D*, 22). Once again, the male is associated with movement and action whereas the female can only await his return; the level of choice is once again heavily weighed in favor of the male, just as in a broader context it is the colonizing power that has the choice of traveling to a new colony or not: the same choice is not open to a colonized people who suddenly find themselves occupied by an invading army.

Throughout *Dubliners* there is a theme of women as repressed by their culture. One thinks of the slavey in "Two Gallants"; one thinks of nanny and Eliza in "The Sisters"; one thinks of the strong-minded Mrs. Kearny in "A Mother"; the list could go on. What these stories demonstrate is that the subject-position of women is very different from that of men. There is a further strain of the enunciation of an alternate female subjectivity that can be traced through Joyce as well; as he endeavors to give voice to the distinctive sense of womanhood that is to be found in all cultures, this line could be traced from Mrs. Mooney in "A Boarding House," through Molly Ivors and Gretta Conroy in "The Dead," through various images of woman in *A Portrait of the Artist as a Young Man*, through perhaps the apotheosis of this trope, Molly Bloom in *Ulysses*, culminating in the almost multigendered *Finnegans*

Wake, where he speaks about being keen "on that New Free Woman with novel inside. I'm always as tickled as can be over Man in a Surplus by the Lady who Pays the Rates" (*FW*, 145, 29–31).

In this book he can aim to unravel the seeming essences of gender: "Male and female unmask we hem" (*FW*, 590, 24), a position that is a long way from Eveline holding onto the iron rails at the North Wall or Mangan's sister holding onto the railings outside her own house in "Araby."

From the perspective of the postcolonial paradigm, what this kind of reading of *Dubliners* can demonstrate is that within the postcolonial experience there are many individual and particularist strands that can be followed. Joyce complicates any sense of totality within that paradigm by demonstrating that the subjectivity of women in *Dubliners* is vastly different from that of their male counterparts. As Howes and Attridge accurately summarize in *Semicolonial Joyce* (2000), although postcolonial scholarship needs to use universalizations and generalizations, they nevertheless sit uneasily with the paradigm's ongoing critique of such universalisms and with its ongoing focus on the particular and the local. As we have seen, Joyce's work is a point of critique and contact between the different tensions of the postcolonial. By focusing on his presentation of women's role, the strength of the postcolonial paradigm, that form of immanent critique that can inhabit societally constructed and ideologically motivated discourses but at the same time offer them to critique, is foregrounded. "Dubliners" as a homogenous grouping, the subject of so much academic criticism, deconstruct before our eyes into different, local, and marginalized individuals. And, as Howes and Attridge argue:

> It is postcolonialism's struggle with the issues raised here, and the difficulties presented by the Irish case, that make the crossroads between these lines of enquiry and Joyce's works, which famously favour questions over answers, a rich ground for further investigation. (Attridge and Howes 2000, 13)

3

Hard Facts and Fluid Spaces

"Ithaca" and the Imperial Archive

JON HEGGLUND

POSTCOLONIAL READINGS of *Ulysses* have had remarkably little to say about "Ithaca."[1] This lack of commentary seems surprising, given the structural importance of the chapter as both the long-awaited homecoming to the "odyssey" of the novel and the leave-taking of two of the novel's major protagonists, Leopold Bloom and Stephen Dedalus. I see two reasons for this relative silence. First, in contrast to chapters that explicitly treat questions of British imperialism and Irish nationalism, such as "Telemachus," "Cyclops," and "Circe," "Ithaca" does not contain a significant amount of content that directly addresses the colonial relations between Great Britain and Ireland. Rather, the chapter narrates, in the form of 309 questions and answers, the return of Bloom and Stephen to the Bloom household, the forced entrance of Bloom into his house (he has forgotten his key), the taking of a cup of cocoa by both men, the departure of Stephen, a brief exchange between Bloom and Molly, and finally the solitary reflections of Bloom as he prepares for and drifts off to sleep. As these homely details suggest, "Ithaca" seems to represent a retreat from the public sphere of politics, culture, and history toward the everyday, familial rituals of the domestic sphere, a space frequently obscured from postcolonial criticism and theory. Second,

1. In two of the pioneering book-length postcolonial studies of Joyce's work, Cheng (1995) and Duffy (1994), "Ithaca" is granted a total of six pages of sustained commentary between both texts. In Attridge and Howes (2000), "Ithaca" merits only two passing references.

the chapter has generally been discussed with reference to its style, or lack thereof. As Karen Lawrence has argued, "Ithaca" is a "radical attack on the idea of literary style," as it "dons the anti-literary mask of science" (Lawrence 1980, 559). Even postcolonial readings of this chapter have tended merely to underscore such oppositions. Vincent Cheng, for example, states that the form of "Ithaca" reveals "specific facts and objective details" that are neither "slanted by an individual stream of consciousness . . . [nor] exaggerated through stylistic parody or fantasy" (1995, 241). Cheng takes the factualism of "Ithaca" at face value, refusing to grant that the apparently objective "anti-style" of "Ithaca" is ultimately yet another stylistic choice.

If we grant that "Ithaca" is as stylistically and formally marked as any of the other chapters in *Ulysses,* then we need to look carefully at the politics of its form. In its "objective" arrangement of questions and answers, the chapter presents itself as a repository of value-neutral facts unmediated by any subjective perception or overt formal parody. Yet, just as "Aeolus" parodies journalistic writing and "Nausicaa" parodies the language of women's magazines and sentimental novels, "Ithaca" too is a parody of a particular mode of representation. In its organization of narrative knowledge into a series of discrete empirical facts, "Ithaca" mimics the structure through which knowledge about colonial territories was organized, managed, and disseminated within British imperial culture in the nineteenth and early twentieth centuries. By suggesting that the world can be rendered as a series of irrefutable and discrete facts, "Ithaca" adopts the form of what Thomas Richards (1993) calls the "imperial archive." The imperial archive, according to Richards, was the imaginative representation of an ideal repository of knowledge through which heterogeneous data about the empire could be ordered and systematized. I read "Ithaca" as a parodic subversion of this formal structure. Throughout the chapter, the pose of objective fact gives way to excessive, disordered, and dubious information that exposes the fluid, ever-shifting nature of the positive knowledge supposedly contained within the archive. Joyce subverts the form of the archive to offer a subtle but unmistakable criticism of an imperial epistemology that constructs colonial space as a static body of knowledge detached from the power relations of imperial rule. In particular, I examine the well-known "ode to water" passage in "Ithaca" as a symbolic countercurrent to the static, fixed geographies of the imperial archive. Beyond the symbolic importance of water as a metaphor for epistemological fluidity, the passage on water also speaks to the particular significance of water in the emerging imperial science of geopolitics. For imperial expansionists, the world's waterways and oceans came to be seen as an extension of land, a territory in its own right. In the passage on water in "Ithaca," however, Joyce offers an anti-imperialist interpretation of water, pointing out its epistemological fluidity and natural resistance to domination and territorialization.

The Imperial Archive, the Irish Survey, and the Topographical Imagination of *Ulysses*

One of the recurring motifs in the study of European imperialism has been a concern with the interrelationships between geography, knowledge, and power (Said 1978, 1994; Driver 1992; Pratt 1992; Edney 1997). In the course of Great Britain's rise to imperial dominance in the nineteenth century, the establishment and administration of colonial territories was largely effected through the systematization and control of knowledge. Thomas Richards refers to the sum total of knowledge about empire—including such diverse forms as exploration narratives, field observations, maps, administrative records, results of scientific experimentation, and other documents—as the "imperial archive." According to Richards, the imperial archive was an imaginative framework within which every bit of information gathered, every piece of data recorded, every specimen collected might be placed and organized. Although the imperial archive was a utopian image whose real manifestations were partial and fragmentary (housed in finite institutional spaces such as museums, record offices, and professional societies), it was a governing fiction of empire because of its ability to provide a conceptual totality for the vast quantities of information being generated by practices such as travel writing, scientific observation, and colonial administration. The key component of the imperial archive, according to Richards, was the discrete, individual fact. In the imaginative structure of the archive, the fact functioned as "raw knowledge . . . awaiting ordering" (Richards 1993, 4). An isolated fact was merely a piece of information, but the idea of the archive promised that such discrete bits of information might be ordered into a comprehensive system of knowledge; that is, "the sense that knowledge was singular and not plural, complete and not partial, global and not local" (7). The archive was thus an epistemological form of forms; it offered a way for every discrete observation and artifact—be it a plant specimen, an observation of cultural practices, or a view of an unfamiliar landscape—to be entered into a unified body of knowledge, which could then be mobilized as cultural power in the service of colonial rule.

Although the imperial archive was ultimately a utopian fiction, its existence was impossible to conceive without reference to a real-world geography. Geography provided a spatial field onto which the heterogeneous data of the archive could be mapped and, therefore, possessed a primary importance in the organization and representation of information about colonial space. In the family of imperial sciences, according to Bruce Avery, geography was "the broad picture, the frame that [situates] the partial vision produced by other sciences" (Avery 1995, 58). For geographers, the archival ideal of singular, unambiguous knowledge was the very foundation of geography's claim to represent the real world. As Matthew Edney points out, geography aimed to produce "a corpus of data, continually growing and correcting itself, its ultimate purpose to encompass and to replicate the real world" (Edney 1999, 170). The most convenient and condensed form of the geographical archive was the map, and it is no accident that the practice of cartography moved away from its early modern association with art toward a rhetoric of scientific and mathematical austerity.[2] Implicit in post-Enlightenment cartography is the idea that each individual map of a specific space can be reconciled to an ideal, totalizing map that replicates the world at a 1:1 scale. Every piece of data, every observation, and every narrative therefore had its proper place on the map, which in theory had a direct mimetic relationship with an actual real-world space. Each discrete piece of data in the imperial archive could therefore be put in its right geographical place by means of cartography. It was no accident, then, that the word "map" came to signify not just a representation of geographical space, but any visual or conceptual hierarchization and ordering of knowledge. As Edney puts it, in post-Enlightenment Europe "the map was widely regarded . . . as the epitome of encyclopedic knowledge" (Edney 1999, 173). Writing of British imperial cartography in

2. For a fuller discussion of the political and cultural reasons for the shift from "artistic" to "scientific" cartographic practice, see Edney (1993).

particular, Edney points out that "maps came to define the empire itself, to give it territorial integrity and its basic existence" (Edney 1997, 2). Maps were not merely neutral representations of imperial territory; by submitting these territories to the common language of latitude and longitude, they forced the heterogeneity and chaos of far-flung colonial places into a seamless graticule of abstract, instrumentalized space.

The discipline of geography, and its corresponding cartographic representations, offered the most persuasive evidence that the imperial archive reflected the existence of comprehensive and positive knowledge about the world. After the "scientific" turn in cartography, which relied upon carefully recorded observations and the mathematical precision of triangulation, there was no room for conflict or dispute on the map. The nineteenth-century turn toward the scientific precision of geography and its utility in supporting the fiction of the imperial archive was perhaps best expressed through the Ordnance Survey of Ireland, undertaken between 1826 and 1852.[3] Along with the contemporaneous Great Trigonometrical Survey of India and subsequent surveys of East Africa, the Ordnance Survey of Ireland, or Irish Survey, as it came to be called, aimed to create a definitive, comprehensive map of a colonial space, wiping away all vestiges of the haphazard, local geographies of towns, estates, and counties. The Ordnance Survey, originally a wing of the British military charged with maintaining supplies and ammunition to troops, became principally responsible for topographical survey and cartography in the late eighteenth century. Setting its sights on Ireland shortly after the Act of Union in 1800, the Ordnance Survey was commissioned to create a comprehensive map of Ireland, scaled at six inches to the mile, for the immediate purpose of providing equitable taxation for property owners on the island, most of whom were Anglo-Irish Protestants. While the explicit rationale for the survey suggested a reasonable, modest aim, the survey was emblematic of a changing conception of imperial space brought about by developments in the science of cartography. The mapping proceeded by trigonometrical survey, or triangulation, which used the laws of mathematics to convert physical terrain into a series of triangles, the exact

3. For the following history of the Ordnance Survey of Ireland, I have relied on Andrews (1975).

locations of which could be determined through the calculation of angles relative to a precisely measured baseline.[4] With triangulation, mapmaking was given the air of epistemological infallibility and scientific precision so central in establishing the modern cultural authority of the cartographic image. Triangulation also fixed any point within the graticule of longitude and latitude that described the shape and size of the globe. By promising a science of location into which any point on the terrestrial earth could be compared with any other point, cartography used trigonometrical survey to create a homogenous global space in which any location could be expressed through two numerical values. The maps of Ireland created by the Ordnance Survey were thus, by definition, part of a uniformly abstract space that was particularly well-suited to rendering the disparate colonies of the British Empire with the common language of latitude and longitude. Like the Great Trigonometrical Survey of India, which was undertaken at roughly the same time and with many of the same technologies and personnel, the Ordnance Survey of Ireland was a part of a larger British imperial project: the systematic and scientific possession of territory by means of codified spatial knowledge.[5]

The Irish Survey succeeded to the extent that the maps produced remained the "official" maps of Ireland until well after independence. Most mass-produced maps from the 1850s until the 1920s were derived from the survey, including those appended to the 1904 edition of *Thom's Official Directory* of Dublin, the legendary source of the topographical detail of *Ulysses*.[6] Although the maps of Dublin in *Thom's* appear ideologically neutral and innocently factual, these maps were in fact derived from an imperial survey of a colonial space. This fact is important not because Joyce's use of these maps somehow implicates him in the colonial domination of his own country, but because *Ulysses* is frequently read according to the

4. For a description of trigonometrical survey, see Edney (1997, 16–25).

5. On the connections between the Great Trigonometrical Survey of India and the Ordnance Survey of Ireland, see Edney (1997, 247–8).

6. The Ordnance Survey began selling its six-inch maps of Ireland to Alexander Thom's publishing house in 1856, four years after the completion of the survey. See Andrews (1975, 228).

spatial assumptions established by post-Enlightenment cartography: that all geographical knowledge fits into one comprehensive archive and that each geographical fact within the archive is empirically positive, existing outside of the observer and independent of the conditions of observation. This approach to the novel, at least in part, seems to have originated from Joyce himself in his famous remark to Frank Budgen: "I want . . . to give a picture of Dublin so complete that if the city one day suddenly disappeared from the earth it could be reconstructed out of my book" (Budgen 1972, 69). Joyce himself would have us believe that his book is as much an archive of geographical fact as it is a narrative of imaginative fiction. If the numbers of scholarly guides to "Joyce's Dublin" are any testimony, literary critics have not actively challenged this understanding of the novel.[7] Readers continue to accord *Ulysses* an epistemological authority akin to that of the map: the novel claims to present a totalizing archive of factual knowledge about Dublin on June 16, 1904.

These readings draw special attention to the importance of topography in the construction of archival knowledge. David Pierce, for example, refers to Joyce's spatial aesthetic as a "topographical imagination" (Pierce 1992, 83). Clive Hart and Leo Knuth have even gone so far as to argue that *Ulysses* is less an adaptation of Homer's *Odyssey* than a rewriting of the 1904 edition of *Thom's Official Directory* of Dublin, the city guide and set of maps from which Joyce gleaned so much of his information during the composition of *Ulysses*. As Hart and Knuth put it, the Dublin of *Ulysses* is not merely the Dublin of Joyce's memory, but also "the Dublin that one may find enshrined, embalmed in the pages of *Thom's*—the official, statistical Dublin, the city reduced to objective memory, to street lists, tradesmen's catalogues, census counts" (Hart and Knuth 1975, 14). Although critics have generally acknowledged that the narrative topographies of *Ulysses* consist of a combination of a factual geography of Dublin and Joyce's fictionalizing imagination, the very separation of these registers implicitly gives epistemological weight to fact over fiction, map over narrative. The map becomes the ground to which the narrative figurations of

7. A sampling of the books about Joyce and *Ulysses* that read the book in terms of its "real-world" geography include Hutchins (1950), Pearl (1969), Hart and Knuth (1975), Delaney (1982), Ellmann (1982), and Pierce (1992).

the novel must inevitably refer. By placing the topography of Dublin within the category of "fact," these readings unwittingly replicate the projection of Ireland as a static object of knowledge rendered up for the disembodied gaze of the observer.

The Fluid Facts of "Ithaca"

If one takes the novel's topographical imagination at face value, then "Ithaca" indeed stands as a logical and fitting end point to this particular stylistic approach. In its question and answer mode, the chapter seems to fulfill the novel's earlier obsession with a spatial mimeticism that renders Dublin as a static geographical archive. The topographical imagination that gives chapters such as "Hades," "Lotus Eaters," and "Wandering Rocks" such a density of detail relies on the assumption that the words of the novel signify a real-world space that actually exists (or at least *existed* on June 16, 1904). Dublin becomes a terra firma, a stable ground onto which Joyce can affix the events of *Ulysses*. "Ithaca" appears to foreground what is implicit earlier in the novel: that fictional narrative does in fact refer to an empirically verifiable world. Through the form of the chapter, Joyce evacuates any pretense of a narrative realism unfolding in time, as the question-and-answer mode presumes a history that has already occurred, the fates of its characters only retrievable as recorded facts. The opening question of the chapter, appropriately, aims to fix the two main characters on a map of Dublin. The questioner asks, "What parallel courses did Bloom and Stephen follow returning?" (*U*, 666.1–2, 17.1). Although literally speaking only of the short walk the two have taken from the setting of the previous chapter, this question effectively boils down the preceding sixteen chapters to their structural essence: an itinerary of the movements of the two major characters throughout the day. The responding narrator—the voice of the archive—gives an answer in a language stripped of all incidentals, reducing and flattening the two characters to moving points on a two-dimensional map of Dublin: "Starting united both at normal walking pace from Beresford place they followed in the order named Lower and Middle Gardiner streets and Mountjoy square, west: then, at reduced pace, each bearing left, Gardiner's place by an inadvertence as far as the farther corner of Temple street, north," and so on (*U*, 666.3–7, 17.2–7). Here, at the beginning of the chapter, we are bound to ask the question: What exactly is the desire of the questioner for such particular pieces of information about these two unassuming Dubliners? And who might these mysterious interlocutors be? Enda Duffy speculates that the form of "Ithaca" recalls "the account of a police investigation with model answers—the transcript of an inquiry that might have taken place, let us imagine, in the interrogation room of the Store Street divisional police station" which Bloom and Stephen passed by in the previous chapter (1994, 181). While, as we shall see, the model of the police interrogation does not hold for the entire chapter, Duffy's speculation points out that the organization of knowledge in this chapter has a peculiarly panoptic feel, as the initial questions suggest a linkage between the possession of knowledge and the exercise of power. Both voices in the chapter assume a faceless, nameless, disembodied authority, whereas Bloom and Stephen are constructed as identifiable, embodied objects of knowledge. Initially, at least, the factualism of "Ithaca" seems less like the value-neutral discourse of science and more like the prison house of colonial surveillance.

If "Ithaca" were able to maintain its "just the facts" pose, this reading of the novel-as-colonial-police might be convincing. But quite early in the chapter, the impossibility of a one-to-one correspondence between question and answer becomes apparent. The solidity of archival fact gives way to the fluidity of information that refuses to be fixed and compartmentalized. Joyce offers another mode of knowledge at cross-purposes with the hermetically closed form of the archive and its imperative to map all facts onto a real-world topography. In response to the topographical imagination suggested by many critics, the novel also offers what might be called a "hydrographic" imagination, through which knowledge overflows its precise boundaries within the archive and on the map. Where the first question of "Ithaca" presumed that Bloom and Stephen could be tracked as discrete points moving through a static space of factual topography, later questions in the chapter suggest that facts might not be as solid and self-contained as the archive demands them to be. As Bloom goes to the stove to heat water for cocoa, the questioner asks, referring to the water, "Did it flow?" (*U*, 671.1, 17.163). Although the question posed only asks for a "yes" or "no" answer, what in fact comes after the initial affirmative response is a lengthy disquisition on the history of the water that flows from Bloom's tap. The answer includes the path the water has taken from the reservoir outside of Dublin, the cost of the pipe carrying the water, the daily amount of water provided by the reservoir, and an account of scandals associated with the Dublin waterworks committee. The archive answers with too much information for the question posed, as facts flow into each other until the initial question appears to have been forgotten altogether. The solid structure of the archive, with its rigid compartmentalization of fact, appears to have sprung an information leak.

This leak becomes a deluge in the next question and answer. The questioner asks, "What in water did Bloom, waterlover, drawer of water, watercarrier returning to the range, admire?" (*U*, 671.26–7, 17.183–4). The question itself is striking. First of all, it calls for a qualitative rather than a strictly quantitative answer, demanding a glimpse into the subjectivity of Bloom rather than the objectivity of the empirically observable material world. Even at the level of language, the necessity of posing an unambiguous, clearly worded question is undercut by the poetic quality of the language used (note the repetition of "water" and the dense consonance of the "w" and "r" sounds). The response is a tour de force of description that becomes less a list of facts than an ode to the mysterious, even mythic force of water. What gives this passage such force, though, is not the use of conventional poetic description to represent the qualities that Bloom ascribes to water, but the encyclopedic collation of disciplinary languages through which water is constituted as an object of knowledge. In describing its "democratic equality," the language of political philosophy is evoked, the reference to Mercator's map calls on cartography, the mention of its depth in the Sundam trench suggests the science of oceanography, and the "restlessness of its waves and surface particles" constitutes it as the object of physics. The passage goes on to evoke the vocabularies of economics, geology, cosmology, climatology, and other disciplines and sciences. Water appears to be the ultimate *inter*disciplinary object of knowledge, flowing effortlessly from one discourse to another, refusing to remain in the discrete, bounded shape of fact. Water even flows over the border between the natural and the human sciences; the answering narrator remarks on "its ubiquity as constituting 90% of the human body" (*U*, 671.28–672.38, 17.185–228). Water even renders the observing human subject as a material object of knowledge. Indeed, as Bloom surmises, water is both "paradigm and paragon" of knowledge in its naturally fluid state (*U*, 672.23, 17.216).

The Geopolitics of Water

Water, then, serves as a convenient symbol for the tendency of facts to overflow their prescribed disciplinary boundaries; knowledge, according to the passage, is more a fluid than a solid medium. But water has more than just a symbolic importance in the context of *Ulysses*: It also possessed a very real geopolitical and historical significance in the history of the British Empire, including relations between Britain and Ireland. Certainly, this significance was not lost on Joyce, as he begins the novel with a scene of tension between the Englishman Haines and Stephen Dedalus at the Martello tower, built by the English to defend against French naval support of Catholic Ireland's desire to restore James II to the throne. For ideologues of British imperial expansionism, the geopolitical control of water was a crucial element in the growth and maintenance of imperial power. As the terrestrial, landed spaces of the world were increasingly parceled out to one imperial power or another, the sea became an urgent theatre of geopolitical competition.

Two writers in particular, Alfred Thayer Mahan and Halford Mackinder, drew attention to the past, present, and future role of water for nations who would establish overseas empires. In his widely influential 1890 book, *The Influence of Sea Power upon History*, Mahan argued that the dominance of island or water-bordered nations is predicated upon how they turn their surrounding waters to national advantage. Great Britain was a textbook example of a nation transforming its waters into an extension of its lands through economic and military control. Because Britain is "so situated that it is neither forced to defend itself by land, it has, by the very unity of its aim directed upon the sea, an advantage as compared with a people one of whose boundaries is continental" (Mahan 1905, 29). Looking at the history of British economic and military expansion, Mahan drew a prescriptive conclusion: when a country is bordered by the sea, "the control of it becomes not only desirable, but vitally necessary" (40). The conquest of water in the name of land-based nations became a necessity in the Darwinian game of imperial competition; the need to stake out strategic ports, passages, and bodies of water moved to the top of the political agenda for aspiring empires. Certainly, the domination of the sea had been recognized as an important component of national strength throughout history. Mahan, however, imagined the sea in a new form that reversed its role as the empty, interstitial space between land masses. Significantly, Mahan begins his description of the sea by likening it to the topography of "a wide common, over which men may pass in all directions, but on which some well-worn paths show that controlling reasons have led them to choose certain lines of travel over others" (25). After Mahan, then, the sea was conceptually and metaphorically an *extension* of land.

Halford Mackinder, one of the pioneers of modern geography and geopolitics, applied some of Mahan's insights in his 1902 geography textbook, *Britain and the British Seas* (note that even the title annexes the oceans to British territory). In describing the geographical position of Britain as an explanation of its rise to world hegemony, Mackinder posits a kind of cognitive paradox whereby the British Isles are at once bounded *and* extended by the sea. "Britain," Mackinder writes, "is possessed of two geographical qualities, complementary rather than antagonistic: insularity and universality. Before Columbus, the insularity was more evident than the universality. . . . After Columbus, value began to attach to the ocean-highway, which is in its nature universal. Even the great continents are only vast islands and discontinuous; but every part of the ocean is accessible from every other part" (Mackinder 1902, 11). Here, Mackinder implicitly addresses the widespread concern that British imperial expansionism was attenuating the primordial, insular identity of "Englishness"; he argues, on one hand, that the sea sets the islands of Britain apart from other nations, but on the other hand, the maritime extension of Britain enables the island nation to be at the same time "universal." Through possession and control of the world's seas, the "national character" of British insularity is extended throughout the globe, allowing the British Empire to both retain its particularity, cast as inward-looking, local "Englishness," and to justify its imperial project in the name of the "universality" granted by access to the sea. Mackinder thus uses the quasi-scientific language of physical geography to provide political legitimation for the extension of empire.

In the specific case of Ireland, Mackinder claims the British right to possession of Ireland as a natural result of their geographical relationship. "The

Irish Sea," he writes, "is a British Mediterranean, a land-girt quadrilateral, wholly British, whose four sides are England, Scotland, Ireland, and Wales" (Mackinder 1902, 20). Here, Mackinder notes the geometrical power of the Irish Sea to unify the "four nations" of Great Britain. The possession of Ireland as a colony of the British Empire is justified not by any ideological or cultural pretense, but simply by the need to retain the abstract geometrical symmetry that appears on the map. Because the Irish Sea organizes Great Britain into a neatly symmetrical image, it follows that not only the sea, but all the lands that border it, including Ireland, *must* be "wholly British." The shape of the sea provides the most persuasive argument for the possession of its surrounding lands under the British flag. This transformation in the understanding of the sea from an empty void to a territorial space in its own right is characteristic of what Stephen Kern refers to as the "positive negative space" of modernism; that is, space that "was formerly regarded as negative now has a positive, constitutive function" (Kern 1983, 153). In a sense, the former vision of the sea as a blank space from which land masses appeared as positive entities has given way to a confusion of this clear figure-ground relationship. As Christopher GoGwilt puts it, Mackinder's pairing of "Britain" *and* the "British Seas" as equally significant spaces suggests that, for the discipline of geopolitics, "land and sea must both be grasped as potentially figure or ground" (GoGwilt 2000, 34).

The geographical importance of water is, fittingly, one of its aspects admired by Bloom. What Bloom admires about the geography of water, however, is not its ability to be channeled to the imperial motives of a specific nation, but precisely its resistance to such territorializations. The first quality listed in Bloom's admiration of water is its "universality." Clearly, "universality" for Bloom (and for Joyce) means something quite different from Mackinder's sense of the word. For Mackinder, the "universality" of the ocean is not at all antagonistic to British insularity; in fact, universality becomes a natural extension of the self-contained island nation. In the "Ithaca" passage, however, the universality of water is implicitly opposed to the particularity of nations and empires; its "preponderance of 3 to 1" gives it a clear superiority to the land surface of the globe. This geographical dominance of water over land, particularly in the Southern Hemisphere, which contained the majority of British colonies, reverses the British imperial view of the significance of the world's waters as an extension of imperial territory. Bloom's thoughts also note the "vastness" of water as represented in Mercator's cartographic projection. This would have been the standard projection for British-produced maps of the world. It was widely used in part because it placed England at the center of the image, and because its distortions made lands in the extreme Northern and Southern Hemispheres appear larger than actual size; this had the advantage of giving increased visual prominence to British possessions such as Canada, Australia, and portions of southern Africa. In short, the Mercator projection exaggerated the extent of the British Empire. What Bloom notices about the Mercator projection, however, is not the preponderance of British red, but of ocean blue. The true empire on which the sun never sets is the empire of ungovernable water, representing in its physical nature "democratic equality," unable to be dominated by the arbitrary boundaries of any land or nation. Not only does water resist territorialization by specific national interests, with its "slow erosions of peninsulas and islands," it ultimately triumphs over any island nation that would seek to master it (*U*, 672.2–3, 17.198).

Taken in the context of the British imperial obsession with the conceptual and territorial control of maritime space, Joyce's catalogue of water in "Ithaca" assumes a multilayered significance. In its overflowing data and detail, it frustrates the epistemological basis of imperial knowledge: that knowledge can be organized in discrete facts, each directly accessible through linguistic and numerical representation. In its specific commentary on its "democratic equality" and geographical dominance, the catalogue also questions, however subtly, the legitimacy of Britain's claim to the world's waterways. Finally, the discourse on water offers a corrective to the topographical, positivist orientation of much criticism about *Ulysses.* Certainly, topography matters; the terra firma of land and territory is of necessity the ground on which the majority of the political and cultural struggles of colonialism take place. But water, as Joyce was well aware, had its own role to play in the drama of postcolonial nationhood. Water was both a conduit for the linkage of cultures as well as a means of escape from the dead-end conflict between British imperialism and Irish nationalism, both of which were committed to a political and cultural identity based on the insular logic of the land.

Conclusion

The firm, stable ground of topography is by no means the only mode of spatial representation in Joyce's work. As Robert Day Adams argues, "The idea of water, being an infinity of things, doing an infinity of things, dominated Joyce's creation" (Adams 1996, 7). Adams traces the significance of water from *Dubliners* to *Finnegans Wake,* pointing out the ubiquity and complexity of water as a dominant symbolic current in Joyce's work. This hydrographical imagination continually washes up against the firm topographies of *Ulysses.* In the "Telemachiad," for example, the margins of Dublin Bay and the Irish Sea yield a reversal of perspective from a land-based to a sea-based vision of Ireland. "Telemachus" takes place in the seaside Martello tower inhabited by Buck Mulligan, Stephen Dedalus, and the Englishman Haines. As Mulligan reminds Haines, the towers were built by Billy Pitt "when the French were on the sea" (*U,* 17.36–7, 1.543–44); that is, when the French were supporting the Irish revolutionary movement of 1798. The towers functioned as British defenses against a French landing on Irish soil, thus drawing an impenetrable barrier between land and water, between the territory forcibly controlled by Great Britain and the open, contested waters of the Irish Sea. The tower only reminds Stephen of his own condition of bondage, as he remarks to Haines that he is "the servant of two masters," the British Empire and the Catholic Church (*U,* 20.27, 1.638).

Two chapters later, in "Proteus," however, Stephen has escaped the prison of the tower and wanders along Sandymount Strand, an immense tidal basin that forms a mile-wide boundary between the city and Dublin Bay. In 1904, Sandymount Strand was less a beach than a flat of land extending to an imperceptible merger with the sea, hardly a defensible, demarcated border. In this stroll along the margins between water and land, the cultural significance of the sea is reversed, going from the claustrophobic medium that hems Ireland, and Stephen, into its colonial prison, to a means of extension and connection that cannot be circumscribed fully by the colonial domination of Great Britain. Notably, Stephen begins to imagine an Ireland shaped by the cultural linkages provided by the sea.

> Galleys of the Lochlanns ran here to beach, in quest of prey, their blood-beaked prows riding low on a molten pewter surf. Danevikings, torcs of

> tomahawks aglitter on their breasts when Malachi wore the collar of gold. A school of turlehide whales stranded in hot noon, spouting, hobbling in the shallows. Then from the starving cagework city a horde of jerkined dwarfs, my people, with flayer's knives, running, scaling, hacking in green blubbery whalemeat. Famine, plague, and slaughters. Their blood is in me, their lusts my waves. I moved among them on the frozen Liffey, that I, a changeling, among the spluttering resin fires. (*U*, 45.10–20, 3.300–8)

In the first two chapters, Stephen is cast into narrow versions of stereotyped Irishness, first by the Englishman Haines, then by his employer, the Ulster Unionist schoolmaster Deasy. Significantly, it takes a walk on the beach—the border between land and sea—for Stephen to imagine a way out of this confinement. While musing on the ocean, Stephen imagines a more suitably protean version of Irishness. This fluidity of imagination extends to the language used to represent Stephen's thoughts. As if to embody the cultural linkages provided by the sea, individual words merge into compounds: "bloodbeaked," "turlehide," "cagework," "whalemeat," and "Danevikings," this last showing that even the overseas conquerors of Ireland were themselves a hybrid people made up of cultural intermixing. Stephen understands his own "blood" to be made up of this fluid mixture, offering a response to the racialist theories of Irish national purity that will be espoused most vocally by the Citizen in "Cyclops."

In his balancing of water with land, the hydrographical with the topographical imagination, Joyce imagines the potential for an Irish identity that avoids both the Scylla of imperial co-optation and the Charybdis of exclusionary nationalism. This conflict, of course, has been repeated tragically over the course of the twentieth century, both in Ireland and throughout the world. By turning to water as a critical space from which both versions of territorialism can be criticized, Joyce finds a "third space" that moves beyond the binary oppositions that seem an inevitable matrix of postcolonial struggle. Joyce perhaps prefigures the critique of Irish nationalism offered in Seamus Heaney's 1969 poem "Bogland," written just as the "troubles" between the Catholic Republic and Protestant Ulster began to intensify into the violent struggle of the past thirty-plus years. Heaney's poem tells of the discovery of centuries-old artifacts and corpses preserved in the moist peat bogs of Ireland's interior. Heaney concludes with a geological image of Ireland that shows the leakages in the idea of a nation as a terra firma existing from time immemorial. Heaney concludes that the bogs of Ireland "might be Atlantic seepage." Then, moving from possibility to certainty, the speaker proclaims of Ireland that its "wet center is bottomless" (Heaney 2001, 658). Heaney offers a striking cultural countermyth, a vision of an island nation whose very core is made up of the mixture of land and sea rather than a strict division between the two. In contrast to conventional British images of the bounded island nation—think of white cliffs, island fortresses, and precious stones set in silver seas—Heaney gives us the island nation as swamp, under perpetual assault by the churning waters of the Atlantic. This image of Ireland as a swampy composite of island and sea counters the preoccupation with land typically shared by both territorial imperialism and postcolonial nationalism. In its messy conglomeration of muddy land and murky water, Heaney's bogland might also be an appropriate metaphor for the kind of epistemological fluidity that takes place within the archive of "Ithaca." The imperial archive, embodied in secure, confined spaces such as the library or museum, was to be a safe house for knowledge, a utopia that could preserve representations of the world even after the world itself had crumbled away. But, as Joyce and Heaney remind us, the signifiers used to fix the world in a coherent image, be they linguistic or graphic, a narrative or a map, are never as bounded and closed as they need to be. Outside of the hermetically sealed world of the archive are the boglands in which the struggles of history and geography take place, and where facts refuse to keep their shape.

Mr. Leopold Bloom, Staunch Britisher

The Problem of Identity under Colonialism

TREVOR WILLIAMS

I WANT TO EXAMINE THE PASSAGE in Circe (*U,* 15.718–855) where Bloom is accused by the Watch of—of what? It is never made clear, although the Watch does say that he was caught "Unlawfully watching and besetting" (15.732–33). All he has done (and the Watch catch him at it) is feed a mangy dog with the pig's foot and sheep's trotter (17.1470–71) that for some strange reason he has recently, late at night, bought. (Part of the problem in dealing with the Circe chapter is that one can never be quite sure what is real and what is fantasy. Did Bloom really buy this pig's foot to complement, late in the day, his early morning purchase of pork kidney? Whatever the answer, the pork purchase by a supposed Jew is a stark reminder of the problem of identity raised everywhere in *Ulysses* and in particular in the passage under consideration here.)

He is accused, basically, of being Bloom, of being who he is. They ask for his name and he proceeds to give them several false identities: first, he is "Dr Bloom, Leopold, dental surgeon" (15.721) and by way of further identity, he is the cousin of "von Blum Pasha" who has "umpteen millions" and "owins half Austria" (15.721–22). He claims legitimacy by referring to his London club "the Junior Army and Navy" (15.730). He hints that he is a naval officer ("It's a way we gallants have in the navy" [15.743]) and a few lines further on he is a doctor ("We medical men" [15.761–62]).

At this point, Martha Clifford appears, calling him "Henry! Leopold! Lionel! (15.753) and demanding that he "clear [her] name" (15.754). Why is Martha in the book at all? Who is she? Is the letter she writes in Lotos-Eaters (5.241–59) really a reflection of her intellectual ability or is it a clever concealing of her real self? Who *is* this Martha Clifford who has subtlety enough to know what Henry Flower wants in the way of correspondence. He is now put in the witness box and stands accused of some vague misdemeanor connected to his relationship not only with Martha Clifford but to all women.

Bloom testifies in his own defense and claims to be "misunderstood," to "being made a scapegoat of," and to being a "respectable married man" (15.776–77). Then he makes, under pressure perhaps, an extraordinary claim in this statement: "My wife, I am the daughter of a most distinguished commander" (15.777–78). Now, Bloom is indeed the son-in-law of old Tweedy (promoted by him for the benefit of the Watch to the rank of "Majorgeneral" [15.779]), but what is interesting about his slip of the tongue here is how closely he has merged his identity into Molly's. It is not that Bloom does not know who he is, but rather that in a marriage there is a merging of identities from the very fact that the couple are indeed a couple, like Siamese twins. But beyond that, we are receiving a living demonstration of the overdetermination of identity, the numerous strands that go to make up the person or ego we think we are.

For Joyce, this question of identity was never idle speculation. Was Joyce Irish? or British? or European? He lived in the ramshackle (as he called it) Austro-Hungarian empire and thus could see at first hand the multiple identities of the subjects of that empire. One thing we can be fairly certain of is that the figure we name James Joyce today would have been a very different kind of writer had he stayed in Ireland all his life. Technically we have to admit that from a legal point of view James Joyce was British; as a subject of the British empire he carried a British passport. That this is a problem for someone subject to imperial control can easily be deduced from Stephen's conversation with Haines in Telemachus, where Stephen very bluntly and uncompromisingly asserts that he is a servant of several masters, one of which is "the imperial British state" (1.643). Presumably, at the end of *Ulysses,* Stephen, like Joyce himself, chose to leave Ireland and avoid the immediate political decisions that staying would have entailed for anyone with a sensitive conscience about the question of the British presence in Ireland.

This question of national identity affects anyone brought up in the shadow of imperialism. Speaking personally for a moment, I can identify very closely with Stephen's relation to Haines. Having lived the first nineteen years of my life in a very homogeneous community in North Wales, I was surprised, in my naïveté, to discover when I went to university in England, that my English friends regarded me as "Welsh" and therefore as different from themselves. Whereas my friends regarded me as Welsh, I simply looked upon them as students or people, without putting a particular label on them. However, I did very quickly wake up to the presence in the imperial heartland of England of what has since been theorized as the Other (with a capital O). Suddenly, I (along with Jews, Turks, Greeks, West Indians, East Indians, and all the other minorities whom England had allowed into the nest) was part of that Other. It did not affect my daily life, as far as I can remember, but as I have grown older, I have become increasingly attuned to this question of how one relates to the Imperial Presence when one is oneself only the Other. Strangely, the Welsh Examination Board, which set the curriculum for Welsh schools, reinforced this "otherness" by assigning less than 10 percent of the history and literature curriculum to Welsh subject matter. My lessening naïveté has arisen from my immigration to Canada, where for many years I have learned how constrained is political life when one lives next door to an imperial colossus. In some ways therefore, my life in Canada has mirrored my life in Wales. For the most part, the only Americans I know personally are the very nice people I meet at Joyce conferences, and because these people tend to be very liberal and embarrassed by America's imperial status, I rarely meet individual Americans with whom I have to engage in the way that Stephen engages with Haines in the first chapter of *Ulysses.*

That conversation between Haines and Stephen raises the question of identity in a raw and direct form. Just before they talk, the old woman has brought milk for the three young men in the Martello tower. It is clear from what Stephen thinks about her that we are to see her as a symbol of Ireland itself. He recalls the names that Ireland has called itself in the darkest days of violent English control and thus draws attention to the importance of names and the slippery nature of identity. But perhaps the most telling moment in that early scene is when Haines the Englishman speaks Irish Gaelic to her (*un*quoted by the multilingual Joyce, who had no command over his native language). She thinks it is French, but that is, I submit, a very embarrassing moment: not to be able to recognize the language of the very country one is supposed to be symbolizing is surely a deep humiliation. Haines is utterly triumphant in this scene and is pleased to proclaim his identity in the simple declarative phrase: "I am an Englishman" (1.430).

When Haines pushes Stephen into discussing belief, he, though intelligent enough to learn Gaelic, is too blind to see where his casual remarks about freedom of belief are leading. Stephen immediately "reads" Haines politically and challenges him to look *parallactically* (an important concept in *Ulysses*) at his own position as symbolic Englishman. As Stephen openly declares his colonialist status, he blushes ("his color rising" 1.643), and the blush comes perhaps not so much from the excitement of the argument as from the fact that he is personalizing the issue, forcing Haines to see that, decent and well-meaning chap though he may be, he is nevertheless a representative of the English exploitation of the Irish. Now Haines himself is an innocent enough character, but perhaps Joyce means us to look a bit closer at what Haines symbolically represents. We learn earlier in Telemachus that Haines's father earned his "tin by selling jalap to Zulus or some bloody swindle or other" (1.156–57). We don't necessarily have to believe Mulligan's gossip, but where there's smoke there's fire, and we can probably deduce that Haines is able to live comfortably here on his Irish field trip precisely because his inherited personal wealth has been amassed in the course of colonial exploitation.

It takes a lot of courage in personal relationships to confront an acquaintance in the way that Stephen does Haines (and without the aid of liquor to fire him up). And yet, the personal is a necessary site of political action, the place where the task of raising consciousness begins. Stephen in effect is saying to Haines, "You, Haines, own me, and therefore I am not free. I may be, as I said a few minutes ago, a 'horrible example of free thought' (1.625–26), but even though I am free to think whatever I like, as all people everywhere are, I am not free to express that thought so long as censorship exists to guard against 'free thought.'"

Haines is no fool and knows that he is being attacked as symbolic Englishman, because he evades the issue by waffling on about "history" being to blame, and a few moments later he has become, not "an Englishman" as he confidently asserted a half hour before when bantering with the milk woman, but merely the much vaguer "Britisher" (spreading the blame around among the Welsh and Scots, in other words). The main point to be made from the analysis of this scene in Telemachus is that Joyce is drawing our attention severely to a real problem for someone who lives as a colonial subject—namely, how *does* one relate to the colonial oppressor on a personal level (to say nothing of the public level)? Who *are* you, really, if you do not "own" your own country? These questions plague politics throughout the ages, often violently. It seems surreal to those of us who live in a more or less democratic peace in countries throughout the European Union and North America to see the action that has recently taken place in Iraq. Always, the same issue is at the heart of these conflicts: Who owns what? Where does one have the right to live? And always, always, that ultimate question of the modern era: Who am I?—a question often answered simply in terms of nationality or class or gender or color or religious affiliation. The categories seem to offer certainty, even security, and yet, as Joyce knew so well, without some leap of faith (itself a potentially dangerous gesture for those not likewise leaping) there is only the "incertitude of the void" (17.1015).

Let us return to the Bloom of Circe, a chapter all the more instructive for the reader because it brings to the surface so much that has been repressed not only on this one day but in the construction of the identity precariously known as "Bloom." When he tries to claim kin with Molly's father, Major Tweedy, he refers to him as "one of Britain's fighting men who helped to win our battles" (15.779–80). The only word I am curious about in that sentence is "our." Does it mean that Bloom, his colonial identity cast aside (to say nothing of his subidentity as Jew), has been interpellated so thoroughly into the ideology of Britishness that he has no difficulty using the word "our," which so cements his identity to the British cause? Probably not, because it is merely a strategy to avoid persecution by the Watch. Nevertheless, the mere fact that he *has* to adopt this particular strategy, involving assertion of his loyalty to the British cause, indicates the problematic of identity for a colonized person.

Having identified himself via his wife and father-in-law and the British cause generally, he now comes closer to home and claims, more specifically, that his regiment was the Royal Dublin Fusiliers, following this up with a list of hilarious clichés to describe these sterling troops "in the service of our sovereign" (15.788–89). Along with the Metropolitan police, they are the "guardians of our homes." I want to return to the different concepts of "home," but for the moment will simply note in passing that it is a word that begs all kinds of questions for a colonized people. Above all, does one, if one's country is "owned" elsewhere, have a home to rule *in*?

A "Voice" then calls out to accuse Bloom of "booing Joe Chamberlain," the British Minister for the Colonies, when he visited Ireland during the recent Boer War. Bloom, we should recall, was "swept along" in a demonstration by medical students against Chamberlain when he came to Trinity College to pick up an honorary degree. Bloom's recollection of this incident in Lestrygonians is interesting for his cynical appraisal of the superficiality of the students' protest: "Few years' time [he predicts] half of them magistrates and civil servants. War comes on: into the army helterskelter" (8.438–39). Despite his clarity of insight here, he nevertheless has found himself caught in an ideological trap: if you do support the British, you will also have to take on board their current imperialistic ventures. In this case, it means *not* supporting a minority (the Boers) who threaten British commercial interests in the Rand. So, Bloom's presumed instinctive sympathies as Jew and Irishman for the Boers is compromised by his need to prove, under duress, his pure Britishness. Which way does one move in these circumstances? In an atmosphere of threatening jingoism, the ordinary citizen will find it difficult to question his or her country's latest military adventure when an oppositional stance puts at risk the very sense of identity that derives from nationhood.

Luckily for Bloom, he does not, in this text that acts out the repressed in an hallucinatory chapter, need to make a decision that has immediate and drastic consequences. Nevertheless, such personal decisions as to one's "true" identity were to remain an active ingredient of Irish politics for many years. And it has a truly pernicious effect, because it leads to the most divisive question of all: who has the True Irish identity? Is it (in 1922) the Free State supporters or the Republicans?

Bloom continues his attempt to inscribe himself within the British ideological hegemony by first claiming that his old dad was a J.P., and then by claiming to be a "staunch Britisher" (15.793–94). These six lines (15.793–98) are fascinating for the way they entangle Bloom's defense of his identity with the broad imperialist themes introduced in Telemachus. If his old man had indeed been a Justice of the Peace, he would have been a dispenser of British justice, an upholder of the centuries' old system of land ownership. Then, his claim to be a "Britisher" links him to Haines when the latter was trying in Telemachus to defuse collective racial guilt for imperialist atrocities by invoking history and reversing his immediate identity from "Englishman" to the more vague and inclusive "Britisher."

Bloom then mentions (15.795) "the absentminded" war. This appropriation (a word I want to use advisedly) of "absentminded" here is interesting, because Bloom himself cannot know where this word has come from in the topography of *Ulysses*. In Scylla and Charybdis, Mr. Best has drawn attention to the way *Hamlet* has been advertised in a French provincial town, it being not simply *Hamlet* but *Hamlet ou Le Distrait, Pièce de Shakespeare* (9.118–21). Stephen translates "le distrait" as "absentminded beggar." This gentle banter all takes place while Stephen inwardly contemplates the truly murderous themes of *Hamlet*: "Sumptuous and stagnant exaggeration of murder" (9.129). He pursues the image of murder into his own time: "Khaki Hamlets don't hesitate to shoot" he pronounces. "The bloodboltered shambles in act five is a forecast of the concentration camp sung by Mr Swinburne" (9.133–35).

It is difficult to see how Joyce could ever have been accused of being apolitical when his novel throws up passages like this, patterns so intricate in their design, yet obvious when one picks at the threads. As this passage suggests, history for Joyce was not something one "blamed" while looking the other way, but rather, as Stephen himself says, a "nightmare," which Bloom in the passage we are mainly considering here had to live out. Joyce (or rather Stephen) makes it easy to draw out political meanings from such a text, starting with the explicit reference to the concentration camp. For us that phrase has entered into our own nightmare of history, a phrase with iconic immediacy. But at the time *Ulysses* was being written the phrase would not have had such resonance, even though the concept had caused considerable opposition in liberal quarters in Britain when Kitchener in 1900 began the policy of confining the women and children of the Boers in these unsanitary camps where 20,000 died. The phrase "deliberate genocide" was used by the Boers to describe this condition, and if we are "shocked and awed" by the pictures in 2003 of burning houses in Baghdad, let us not forget that it was Lord Kitchener who invented a thing called the "scorched earth policy" as his way of denying the claims of the Boers to run their own show in their own land.

The intricate weave of *Hamlet* within *Ulysses* remains interesting no matter how often the connection is revisited. When one steps back from the cloying claustrophobic intensity of Shakespeare's play, with its focus on the agonized individual psyche, the picture that emerges in the *long* view is of a society in which spying is seemingly the natural order of things, where no one's identity is quite certain: is Hamlet mad or not? is Ophelia chaste or not? was King Hamlet really murdered by Claudius? what is the difference between Guildenstern and Rosencrantz? is Polonius a kindly wise old man or an interfering irresponsible patriarch? And in the background, one can smell the rottenness that is the state of Denmark, a state whose identity will be snuffed at the end of the play by an invasion of Norwegian troops. For Stephen, I think, *Hamlet* is the one play of Shakespeare that provides the objective correlative of Ireland's condition. (It was of course T. S. Eliot who used this term to describe the *in*ability of *Hamlet* to fulfill its author's intent—the objective action of the play did not match the depth of emotion felt by the playwright in the moment of composition). Not for the first time in his life, Eliot got it wrong, for surely *Hamlet* does enact perfectly the one condition that Joyce understood so well: paralysis. Just as Homer's *Odyssey* provides the skeleton on which to flesh out an ordinary Dublin day, so too does *Hamlet* make possible the rendering of this otherwise uninteresting subject.

Paralysis, as everyone knows, is the major theme of Joyce's work. For someone raised in a colony, this preoccupation with paralysis is perfectly understandable, that being the daily experience of the colonized subjects. You have plenty of freedom to come and go and to make a living (especially if you can find a job linked to the imperial administration or, like Mulligan, you are a member of the professional classes), so much freedom that, if the imperial presence does not, for whatever reason, resort to violence too often to enforce its hegemony, you can for long periods forget that the soldiers are there; you can even forget that your ability to make decisions and decide who you are and who you may become is ultimately controlled in some foreign metropolis.

In other words your life has been appropriated. Joyce knew about appropriation, for in *Ulysses* he played around constantly with the concept of linguistic ownership. Who owns the words we speak? And does it matter? When Bloom says he was in the "absentminded war," the text, on Bloom's behalf (for Bloom cannot surely be aware of his linguistic theft), is demonstrating the process of appropriation. This is appropriation of a positive kind, well illustrated in Scylla and Charybdis, where Joyce appropriates Shakespeare's language and re-presents it for his own purposes. In effect, Joyce is demonstrating the workings of linguistic and literary history, a process that develops eventually into a new language (as perhaps is the case in *Finnegans Wake*). Once Shakespeare's language has gone into public circulation, those who follow after him are free (barring copyright restraints or outright censorship) to use his language any way they choose. *Ulysses* continually demonstrates this positive appropriation. (A famous example is the phrase "retrospective arrangement," which starts off as Tom Kernan's in Hades [6.150], but then wanders into several domains as the novel progresses, becoming now Bloom's phrase and then being taken over by the narrator, who assumes ownership in its last appearance in Ithaca [17.1907], where in describing Jewish migration across Europe it enacts the movement of history itself as a vast "retrospective arrangement," except that this particular rearrangement of the Jews is the harbinger of the nightmare of many murderous forced migrations in the twentieth century.)

Opposed to this "positive" appropriation is a more active, and ultimately negative, process where words or ideas become the linguistic property of a certain group who maintain their own hegemony by their ability to ascribe a single meaning to a particular word or concept. The invention of the term "politically correct" (itself unstable, there being some doubt as to whether it contains within itself some self-directed irony—that is, what started out perhaps as a term of abuse may have stabilized into an expression of a norm) has led occasionally to a kind of cultural terrorism within the academic world. But in the real world, as Noam Chomsky has often shown, it is the norm for certain concepts to be declared acceptable for public discussion and others not.

No one is more aware than Joyce of the way the single word can be misused for political purposes. When Mr. Deasy, the apologist for the Protestant

Ascendancy, says to Stephen, "We are a generous people but we must also be just," the latter's reply is very clear-eyed: "I fear those big words . . . which make us so unhappy" (2.262–64). Stephen seems to spend most of his time in the book divesting himself of ownership in many of its guises, including the linguistic. By the time he leaves the book he is, unlike Bloom, the owner of practically nothing. Bloom himself seems in Hades to assert that ownership is an ambiguous concept, when his interior monologue twice within two pages comes up with the phrase "Nobody owns" (6.333, 365). Bloom's use of this phrase is intriguing. It is not quite clear what he is talking about. The phrase is first inspired by the sight of a pauper's coffin going by, and so there does seem to be a specific context for it, as if the pauper who has died *belongs* to no one in the sense of an ownership entailed in belonging to a family. His second use of it, only minutes later, seems to be inspired by recollection of his father's suicide. Suicide, for those who experience it, that is, for those who are left behind when a family member or friend commits suicide, must involve a radical rupture of this sense of ownership, as if the object that one "owns"—in the *good* sense of "own"—has been forcibly taken away.) The phrase, while explicable in its two contexts, seems to draw attention to itself.

Two points seem worth making: first, it is simply not true that "nobody owns," for even the poorest person, at the most extreme of human poverty, owns *something, some* kind of clothing to cover the body. So we cannot perhaps be talking about the ownership of personal items like houses or jewelry or books or whatever. Even in the most Communist of utopian states in some postnuclear future, personal ownership of this kind would have to remain. No, Bloom may have a larger concept of ownership, perhaps the ownership of material that properly belongs to everyone, such as (or especially) water and land. Bloom's phrase seems to echo a sentiment in Blake's short, angry poem "London" in which he twice in the first two lines invokes the adjective "chartered" to describe first the streets and then the Thames. The word itself is the base on which the superstructure of the social degradation is built. (Who can forget the closing lines: "the youthful Harlot's curse/Blasts the new-born Infant's tear,/And blights with plagues the Marriage hearse." It seems clear to me that Blake wants us to respond, "But how can you *charter* water, how can you legally define an entity by definition so fluid?

Bloom was probably not a reader of Blake, but he certainly expresses the idea behind Blake's poem when in Lestrygonians he wonders, "How can you own water really? It's always flowing in a stream, never the same, which in the stream of life we trace. Because life is a stream" (8.94–96). As usual, when Bloom muses on everyday realities, he is "on" to something, in this case the very concept of ownership itself. Bloom is not saying, in 1904 and with his contemporary political outlook, that monopoly capitalism or imperial conquest are bad for our health, but *behind* Bloom, in the weave of this tapestry of a book, an idea circulates that monopoly ownership of *anything*, whether it be of land or water or ideas or of one country by another, is bound to lead to injustice. And the proof of this assertion, I would submit, is in the very structure of *Ulysses* itself, where no single style is allowed to assert its hegemony. *Why* did Joyce go to such extraordinary lengths to ensure that each chapter was different from another? Perhaps because he was above all a liberal democrat, whose ideal was the plurability of voices. Whether it is Stephen in *Portrait* resisting the various voices that would tie him down like nets, or whether it is the different styles of *Ulysses* or whether it is the babel of voices in *Finnegans Wake,* the aim seems to be identical: to avoid the imperialism of the Cyclopean or one-eyed view, to encourage parallax or the second look, or, as Bloom out of the blue says in Hades, to imagine ourselves as someone else: "If we were all suddenly somebody else" (6.836). Stephen expresses the very same idea in Scylla and Charybdis: "Every life is many days, day after day. We walk through ourselves, meeting robbers, ghosts, giants, old men, young men, wives, widows, brothers-in-love, but always meeting ourselves" (9.1044–46). When Stephen articulates what Bloom only vaguely feels (that he is the servant of two masters) he is pointing to the monolithic power of the state and of the holy Roman Catholic and Apostolic Church to close off debate. Graham Greene was fond of pointing to the similarities between the College of Cardinals and the Politburo of the USSR, but Greene was a subject of neither, whereas Bloom and Stephen are indeed subjects, as was their creator, of monopoly power structures.

And how well Joyce points in the march of the styles of *Ulysses* to the effect of this monopoly power on the individual. From the end of Nausicaa to the end of Ithaca, a total of 293 pages in a book (the Gabler edition) of 641 pages, Bloom disappears under the weight of language and style and technique. Not quite "disappeared," but his consciousness is being filtered back at us, heavily mediated by the sands of language, and always we have to infer from the (often hilarious) superstructural style what banal thoughts are going through Bloom's mind at any given moment. Moreover, this diminishment of Bloom, the individual crushed beneath the weight of a language and structure thoroughly owned elsewhere, is both comic and intensely serious. We can take it either and both ways.

So when we reach the line (15.797) where Bloom says "I did all a white man could," what meaning lies impacted in that deceptively simple claim? Joyce has from Telemachus set up a dichotomy in the Irish landscape between those who have invaded and now own the colony and those who have to take orders and be tamed. The references in that chapter to "the rage of Caliban" (1.143) and to "palefaces" (1.166) are too obvious to miss. Bloom then is using the cliché which expresses so well the white man's effortless historical domination of his political landscape: all a white man could do in these hostile conditions; all the superior expectations that one has of the "superior" white man, that which marks him out from the rest and lends him his nobility. That is one side, the cliché side of the phrase (appealed to in the imperialist writings of Rudyard Kipling, G. A. Henty, and Frederick Marryat). However, the other side has to do with the appropriation of identity. In *Ulysses,* various attempts are made both to fix Bloom's identity (he is a Jew) and simultaneously to deprive him of one (he cannot be Irish, is the implied argument, if he is a Jew). Thus one can say that his identity is appropriated by those around him; it is theirs to give or to refuse. But at the same time, Bloom is himself forced, in this scene, to appropriate an identity, the white man's, which is denied to him by the surrounding society. (I will say nothing here about the fact that Bloom is indeed, literally, a white man, nor will I pursue the paradox that the English regard the Irish in the same way that the Irish regard the Jews) It is an example of a complex interpellation. That is, the dominant or owning class (here the church and the state between them) calls its members into a certain consciousness. How the consciousness of a person living in the Ireland of Bloom is actually constructed is too complex a matter to deal with here, but one can at least mention some of the strands that compete for his attention: the British state apparatus, the Roman Catholic Church, the Protestant Ascendancy, the division within the Irish nationalist movement as to the way forward, the position of the immigrant community, and of course the influence of family and personal relations. Obviously that broad spectrum will produce both a Stephen Dedalus and a Leopold Bloom. But one can hazard a guess that everyone in Dublin would know what the phrase "all a white man could" implied, and that, consciously or not, most people, regardless of their political or religious affiliation, would want to be identified with that meaning.

Yet we, reading Bloom's claim in this context, "know" how to read it, know that we are supposed to reverse it and laugh at this claim that Bloom is a "white man" when he so obviously is not by the criteria outlined above. The same phenomenon is supposed to occur when the "pale-faced" Philip Beaufoy, the author of *Matcham's Masterstroke,* the story that Bloom had read in the toilet in Calypso and had used to wipe himself (an outrageously anticolonialist gesture surely) now comes on stage to make the accusation that Bloom is not a "gentleman." Again, this word has been appropriated by a certain class to denote a certain kind of achievement in human conduct. What does the word "gentleman" connote? At one time in its history it did denote a man of a certain class, just beneath the nobility, and that meaning is still preserved in ceremonial titles connected with the British monarch. In Bloom's day, the word had been watered down to mean a certain quality of behavior, but had also been neutralized to its present status as alternative for the much simpler "man." In cricket it was only in 1962 that the English did away with an annual game between Gentlemen and Players. Gentlemen were those who had private incomes and who could play cricket every summer without payment, while Players were professionals who needed the money, a perfect illustration of a very real class distinction.

Thus, inscribed within the word "gentleman" there is a lot of baggage to do with class. Of course, it would be perfectly feasible to call a *working* class person a gentleman. But when a working class man is being called a gentleman by a member of a higher class, there is an element of condescension to it. ("Despite his class position, he is worthy of being considered one of us.") If a *working* class man were to say of a fellow working class man "he's a gentleman," the phrase would be relatively neutral, but one would still have to wonder to what extent the speaker had taken on board the values embedded by the class system in that word. This word makes an early appearance in

Ulysses. In Telemachus, Mulligan twice (1.51–2 and 155–6) informs Stephen that Haines thinks he is "not a gentleman." What is meant by this term in this context? It is possible that Haines does indeed see Stephen as a lower class kind of fellow. However, I believe another meaning is at work, along these lines: no *gentleman* would be so confrontational, so down to earth in his conversation as to call a spade a spade (as Stephen a half hour later will be doing in his "three masters" speech, which causes Haines some embarrassment). To put it the other way round: a gentleman is someone who will acquiesce in mystification, who will close his eyes to some of the injustices around him, who will not call a spade a spade. To put it even more graphically: the little boy in the Hans Christian Andersen story who exclaims from the crowd that the Emperor wears no clothes is definitely not a gentleman, because he is forcing people to acknowledge what is indeed before their eyes. This forced confrontation with an uncomfortable truth is what emerges from a conception of art as a nicely polished mirror.

When Bloom wipes himself with a page from *Matcham's Masterstroke,* it is in its way a masterstroke of a gesture, and it is seen as such by the author, Beaufoy, here standing in for the British administration and, more generally, for that vague something called Authority. Beaufoy draws attention to Bloom's symbolically defiant gesture when he shows the evidence: "The *corpus delicti,* my lord, a specimen of my maturer work disfigured by the hallmark of the beast" (15.843–45). In other words, Bloom, identified here with the anti-Christ, is aligned with Stephen in his nongentlemanly role of uncovering what many would prefer to remain covered. For Joyce, Stephen and Bloom are characters who stand outside the dominant discourses of their society for a moment and take a second, or parallactic, look at an issue.

It is possible that Joyce clearly foresaw the problems that would ensue from ownership of the means of communication in the twentieth century. Which is why, in the only way he was able as a writer, he demonstrated in all he did that monopoly ownership was disastrous for a civilized society. We may be able to parody certain styles within *Ulysses,* but their radical instability ensures that no one style can purchase a monopoly. In Ithaca, with its relentless pseudoscientific reduction of life to a set of questions and answers, there suddenly emerges that wonderful piece of pure poetry: "the heaventree of stars hung with humid nightblue fruit" (15.1039). And one may praise

Joyce for this sudden irruption of poetry into the midst of the discourse that has come to dominate our century completely.

However, the "second opinion," if we have learnt Joyce's lesson correctly, may involve asking: is there not another way of looking at this poetry? Poetry was once, some seven or eight hundred years ago, a medium totally involved in promoting the hegemony of the secular and religious ruling classes. So much for the purity and apolitical status of poetry. Monopoly ownership is a serious matter, for in the final instance, what happens outside of us, in the society around us, eventually infiltrates our consciousness and helps construct the minds we think we personally own.

I want to conclude by asserting that *Ulysses* really does attend to this construction of the private by the public. Few things are more private than the relationship between two people which we call marriage or, as with Joyce and Nora, simple cohabitation. Moreover, *Ulysses* surely is nothing if not a close examination of the state of matrimony, but not in the farcical manner of the French triangle (which is what Stephen reduces Shakespeare to in Scylla and Charybdis [9.1065]), but in a serious theoretical manner. What part do concepts of ownership play in these relationships? Does one partner own the other? Is there good ownership and bad ownership? Is Bloom testing the limits of ownership within marriage? If one is against monopoly ownership in the larger society, is it a contradiction to have monopoly ownership within the home? Or is it a different kind of ownership? Who rules in the home?

The push toward Home Rule for Ireland was reaching a noisy and violent climax at precisely the moment that *Ulysses* too was nearing its conclusion. The connecting link between these two events may be the notion that ownership of the country has some connection with the way life is conducted in the domestic home. This is not to say, simplistically, that once the English have been driven out, the new civilization of domestic harmony will dawn. But there is a sense in *Dubliners, Portrait,* and *Ulysses* that everything is "on hold" so long as the British keep the country in thrall. Even as late as Penelope a jarring note is introduced when we learn (something that even Bloom himself does not know) that Molly has had an affair with the "so English" (18.889–90) Lt. Stanley Gardner, a soldier in an English regiment (18.389). He called her "my Irish beauty" [18.392] (with its undertones of superior/inferior), but Molly has committed a grave offense by nationalist standards in having sexual contact with him. The point to be strongly made, however, is that private relationships under colonialism are infiltrated with considerations going far beyond the merely sexual.

Joyce's multiplicity of styles in his total oeuvre point the way to a freedom from monocular ways of observing the world associated with imperialism and its monopolistic drive. His texts suggest that such a freedom can only arrive when in the larger political world there is a genuine freedom that does not depend on any one interest group owning more than its fair share of national or international wealth. Although such a hoped-for eventuality may be utopian, merely to use the word "utopian" is an excuse for infinite deferral. If Joyce has taught us nothing else, his own example of slow but determined labor in building a complicated edifice that everyone told him he was crazy to attempt should be the prompt answer to all cries of utopianism.

5

Traveling Ulysses

Reading in the Track of Bloom

WILLIAM C. MOTTOLESE

JAMES JOYCE WAS NOT THE FIRST to write a story of three young men living in Martello Tower in 1904. *Ulysses* begins with a scene already written by an Irish travel writer named William Bulfin. In his *Rambles in Eirinn,* Bulfin visits Martello Tower to find three "men of Ireland" (1907, 323). Bulfin describes one as a traveling Oxford student and "strenuous nationalist" wearing a Gaelic league badge, the second as a poet and Trinity student with the wit of Swift, and the third as a brooding "singer of songs which spring from the deepest currents of life" (323).[1] Joyce, who had read Bulfin's *Rambles* serialized in *Sinn Féin* in 1906 (Joyce 1966, 191), realized that he, Oliver Saint John Gogarty, and Samuel Chevenix Trench were already "folk . . . for [a book]" (*U,* 1.367), represented as certain Irish types in Bulfin's narrative about his bicycle adventures through the Irish countryside. The entire first episode, itself the start of a day of rambles for Stephen, alludes to a scene already written in a travel narrative. From the beginning of *Ulysses,* Joyce appears to be foregrounding travel, especially for those readers who might have read Bulfin. But it is not travel of the mythic variety; rather, it is the kind of touring serious travelers did at the turn of the century.

Bulfin reminds us that Martello tower housed another traveler, Gogarty's friend Trench, a member of an old Huguenot Anglo-Irish family with a history of public life and letters. Interestingly, Trench's great uncle, Francis

1. Richard Ellmann briefly mentions this scene from Bulfin's book (1983, 172–73).

Chevenix Trench, published several travel narratives and a distant cousin, William Steuart Trench, a land agent, wrote the ethnographically rich *Realities of Irish Life* (1868).[2] Enda Duffy (1994, 40–53) and Vincent Cheng (1995, 151–69) have effectively argued that "Telemachus" is an ethnographic episode, in which Haines, the English traveler-ethnographer, initiates an ethnographic encounter with the colonized "wild Irish" Stephen (*U*, 1.731).[3] Haines, however, is less a formal anthropologist than the kind of dilettante ethnographer that most travel writers of the nineteenth and twentieth centuries were. That Joyce transformed Haines from the Anglo-Irish Revivalist Trench into an English traveler suggests that Haines's book would fit into a long tradition of English travel writing about Ireland that goes back to Giraldus Cambrensis in the twelfth century. Thus, a day of wandering by Stephen and Bloom is also a day that will, Haines hopes, take shape in his own travel narrative.

The notion of Joyce and travel brings us back to the early days of *Ulysses* criticism. One of the earliest full studies of *Ulysses,* Stuart Gilbert's *James Joyce's Ulysses* (1955), advances a premise that has almost been lost in Joyce studies: that Leopold Bloom is a traveler. Gilbert cites Victor Berard's *Les Phéniciens et l'Odyssée* (1902–3), an academic study that shaped Joyce's own use of the *Odyssey.* Berard argues that *The Odyssey* is a Hellenic/poetic version of a Phoenician/travel log: "The poem is obviously the work of a Hellene, while the 'log' is clearly the record of a Semitic traveller. The poet—Homer, if you will—was a Greek—Ulysses as, we know him was a Phoenician" (quoted in Gilbert 1955, 82).[4] What Gilbert first emphasized in 1930

2. Also see Gregory M. Downing's "Richard Chevenix Trench and Joyce's Historical Study of Words" (1998). Downing discusses the Trench family, in particular Samuel's prolific grandfather, Richard Chevenix Trench, Archbishop of Dublin and eminent philologist.

3. In the past few years, ethnographic approaches to Joyce have begun to appear. See Gregory Castle's *Modernism and the Celtic Revival* (2001), Marc Manganaro's *Culture, 1922: The Emergence of a Concept* (2002), and William Mottolese's "'Wandering Rocks' as Ethnography? Or Ethnography on the Rocks" (2002). James Buzard in "'Culture' and the Critics of *Dubliners*" (1999/2000) looks at the critical history of *Dubliners* and compares it to Anglo-American cultural anthropological practices of the twentieth century.

4. For a more contemporary analysis of Joyce's relation to Berard's book, see Michael Seidel's *Epic Geography: James Joyce's Ulysses* (1976).

warrants revisiting today: that *Ulysses* is a book about traveling. On a mythic level, Bloom is the Greek Odysseus, an Ithacan insider unable or unwilling to stay home. He is also the Semitic traveler: a Phoenician trader-explorer and seafaring outsider, marooned as a castaway on scattered islands around the Mediterranean; and he is a Wandering Jew, Europe's perpetual outsider trying to find a new promised land.

But Joyce studies has voyaged far from the New and myth critical approaches that dominated *Ulysses* criticism in the mid–twentieth century, when the notion of Bloom as an epic traveler or, to invoke the title of Richard Kain's classic study, a "fabulous voyager" was a guiding critical assumption. Thanks to Edward Said, Mary Louise Pratt , Stuart Hall, and others, "travel" has gained a renewed critical currency, mostly because of the way travel writing has taken part in maintaining colonial and Orientalist discourses, or for James Buzard, how travel writing crystallized moments in the emergence of such key modern concepts as "culture," "the picturesque," "the traveler" itself.[5] Although one new study of Joyce has revisited the epic, very little has been done with travel recently.[6] What I am suggesting is that "traveling *Ulysses*" might prove as fruitful a critical framework as "epic *Ulysses*" or "ethnographic Joyce." My intention in this essay, therefore, is not to make a comprehensive reading of Joyce and travel, but to make a small critical foray that, I hope, will raise more questions than provide answers. What role does travel, of any definition, play in *Ulysses*? How can we read *Ulysses* as a kind of travel log for Bloom? What is the relation of *Ulysses* to travel writing and other nonacademic ethnographic writing? Since *Ulysses* is, in part, a story of travel, what does that say about those who travel and observe (Bloom) and those whom he observes (Dubliners, who observe the observer)? Most of all I want to revive the centrality of "travel" in reading *Ulysses,* by suggesting

5. See especially Edward Said's *Orientalism* (1978), Mary Louise Pratt's *Imperial Eyes: Travel Writing and Transculturation* (1992), Stuart Hall's "Cultural Identity and Diaspora" (1994), and James Buzard's *The Beaten Track: European Tourism, Literature and the Ways to Culture* (1993a).

6. One recent study of note has even revisited the epic in Joyce in terms of nationalism. See Andras Ungar's *Joyce's Ulysses as National Epic: Epic Mimesis and the Political History of the Nation State* (2002).

that travel discourse shapes the novel in significant ways and by focusing on the presence in *Ulysses* of a single travel book, Frederick Diodati Thompson's *In the Track of the Sun: Diary of a Globetrotter* (1893).

❧

As much as Bloom can be read as a mythic traveler, on the narrative's most literal level, Bloom is a very real Irish-Semitic traveler. As "mackerel" the Boer war protestor (*U,* 8.405) and as a reputed confidante of Sinn Féin founder Arthur Griffith (*U,* 12.1574–1577), Bloom evokes the itinerant Fenian leader James Stephens, who in the 1850s traveled Ireland in disguise to study its people and speculate on its future. Bloom is also a Jewish man who wanders around Dublin, always lurking on the fringes of Dublin social life looking in. He is the "dark horse" Throwaway, Gerty MacDowell's "foreigner" with "dark eyes and . . . pale intellectual face" (*U,* 13.415–16), and the "Incog Haroud al Raschid" shrouded in "Caliph's hood" fleeing from the "bloodhounds" and the "night watch" of Dublin natives in "Circe" (*U,* 15.4325–4361). Thus, in "Oxen of the Sun," Joyce gives him the label "traveller Leopold" (*U,* 14.138), and in "Hades," Ned Lambert tells John Henry Menton that Bloom worked for Wisdom Hely's as "a traveller for blotting paper" (*U,* 6.703). In "Sirens," while writing to Martha Clifford, he tells Richie Goulding that he is answering an advertisement to be a "town traveller," (i.e., a traveling salesman) (*U,* 11.887). And in "Circe," the episode of multiple identities, Joyce depicts Bloom in one hallucination as an imperial man: a Victorian traveler and "acclimatised Britisher" who peers into the "loveful households" of Dubliners, seeing in an "urban district . . . scenes truly rural of happiness" (*U,* 15.909–13).

Canvassing Dublin, Bloom does not imagine himself as Odysseus or Moses but as a contemporary traveler. Bloom *is* what he *reads,* and his bookshelf in "Ithaca" shows that he has a genuine interest in travel writing. Thus, as Bloom navigates Dublin's streets, his own thoughts often drift to far-off and exotic places, such as Turkey, Persia, Gibraltar, and Palestine. Bloom's mental globetrotting reveals that even as he moves around Dublin and carefully observes its Dublin social life around him, his thoughts turn to images from popular travel books. In particular, he thinks of Thompson's *In the Track of the Sun* (1893), one of three travel books on his bookshelf; the others are William Ellis's *Three Visits to Madagascar during the Years of*

1853–1854–1856; with Notices of the Natural History of the Country and of the Present Civilization of the People (1858), listed in "Ithaca" as "Ellis's *Three Trips to Madagascar*," and "*Voyages in China* by Viator," an unidentified and probably fictionalized title. In *Ulysses*, Joyce frames Bloom not just as a mythic traveler but as a conventional late-Victorian European traveler.

Despite the orientalism of *In the Track of the Sun*, I do not intend to make an intensive study of the orientalist images that Joyce weaves into Bloom's consciousness.[7] Rather, I argue that Joyce establishes *Ulysses* as a kind of contemporary travel narrative in which the Jewish-Irish Bloom observes and registers life in 1904 Dublin from the margins of the city's dominant and defining cultural group—the mostly Catholic middle class residing mostly on Dublin's north side. As an inside-outsider, he travels along a culture's margin, registering ethnographic observations from a perspective like that of the anthropological participant-observer.

Thinking about Bloom as a real, not mythic, traveler living in the second city of the British empire gives us one way of conceptualizing how Joyce writes ethnographic fiction in *Ulysses*, particularly in the episodes from "Calypso" to "Wandering Rocks." Joyce, the Dublin insider who moves outside Dublin, creates a character who is an outsider living inside city life. As Bloom wanders around Dublin, his consciousness functions as a notebook page on which Joyce can record observations about Dublin life. Bloom typically produces images and observations from *In the Track of the Sun* and other travel narratives in his thoughts in the early episodes. They commonly emerge in counterpoint with or comparison to insights and observations Bloom makes about Dublin life, especially in such ethnographically rich scenes as Bloom's visit to All Hallow's Church in "Lotus Eaters" and Paddy Dignam's funeral procession and burial in "Hades." This juxtaposition of exotic knowledge with Bloom's own ethnographic observations about local life functions in two primary ways. First, it underscores Bloom's position in Dublin life. As an inside-outsider Irish-Jew, he is both familiar and exotic, Hibernian and Oriental, local and worldly. Second, as

7. Regarding Bloom's orientalism, see Duffy's *Subaltern Ulysses* (1994), Cheng's *Joyce, Race and Empire* (1995), Castle's *Modernism and the Celtic Revival* (2001), and *James Joyce Quarterly* 35, no. 2/3 (1998), a special issue devoted to Joyce and Orientalism.

Bloom frames ethnographic observations of Dublin life with observations from travel discourse, he underscores the idea that the Irish themselves are strange to him. Even more, by emphasizing their strangeness to Bloom, Joyce reminds us that throughout the previous centuries, the Irish had been represented in travel writing, ordinance survey documents, journalism, and so forth as odd, exotic, and primitive by both English colonial outsiders and Irish Revivalists. In "Calypso" when Bloom first thinks of *In the Track of the Sun* and produces a chain of orientalist images in his head, he himself questions the validity of "the kind of stuff you read: in the track of the sun" (*U,* 4.99–100), admitting, "probably not a bit like it really" (*U,* 4.99) Likewise, while realistically representing Dublin life in good faith, Joyce will constantly critique his own ethnographic representation. Although the "culture" built especially through the ethnographic realism of the novel's first half remains a significant part of *Ulysses,* Joyce will remind us, particularly in later episodes such as "Eumeaus," of the discursive violence done to the Irish and other peoples represented ethnographically.[8]

The modulation of Bloom's consciousness between local Dublin culture and his imaginings about "exotic" places far afield reflects Joyce's own construction of Irish national identity, itself partially worked out through a dense ethnographic style that shifts between two registers—the local and the worldly.[9] That the "paralyzed" Dubliners of 1904 should inhabit a fictionalized city that Joyce depicts as far more diverse and worldly than they are reflects his characterization of his nation's uneven modernization, an idea that historians (Hechter 1975; Boyce 1995) have used to explain Ireland's development under colonialism. More recently, literary critics such as Marjorie Howes (2000), Luke Gibbons (2000), and Gregory Castle (2001) have begun to explain Joyce's work in this way, through the clash of what Terry Eagleton calls the "archaic" and "avant-garde"—the admixture of traditional

8. See my "Wandering Rocks as Ethnography? Or Ethnography on the Rocks" (Mottolese 2002) for a discussion of Joyce's ethnographic realism in *Ulysses.*

9. The alliance of James Joyce with Irish nationalism beyond a tolerant liberalism would not be possible without significant critical reassessment in the 1990s: in particular, the body of Seamus Deane's work in Irish studies, Emer Nolan's *James Joyce and Nationalism* (1995), Declan Kiberd's *Inventing Ireland* (1996), and the work of Duffy (1994) and Cheng (1995).

and modern elements in Irish modernism (Eagleton 1995, 273–319). Joyce constructs his version of national identity at a time of national emergence and urgent cultural constestation in Ireland (1914–1922)—a point made by Edna Duffy and other postcolonial critics—and lodges it in his depiction of Dublin that is both reflective and projective. *Ulysses* reflects on, assesses, and diagnoses the familiar Catholic lower-middle-class culture that was beginning to dominate Dublin and Irish life in 1904—and had effectively achieved social hegemony by 1922—and simultaneously presents and projects a far more cosmopolitan, diverse, and worldly Dublin. Joyce's ethnographic fiction strives to assess the traditional—the middle-class Catholic Northside culture whose "paralysis" signifies its slow, if not frozen, movement into modernity. It also envisions a new Ireland in which this culture is renewed and reinvented by the cosmopolitan and worldly. Thus, both the traditional and cosmopolitan coexist consubstantially in Joyce's fictionalized Dublin, like Molly's entwined visions of Gibraltar and Howth Head, in the final pages of *Ulysses,* in which she superimposes the diversity and vibrancy of the Rock of Gibraltar ("the Greeks and the Jews and the Arabs and the devil knows who else from all the ends of Europe" [*U,* 18.1587–1589]) upon the iconically Irish familiarity of Howth Head.

As an "internal" colony (Hechter 1975, 9) that in the lore of travelogues and tourist pamphlets, is, likewise, a strange and beautiful place in close proximity to the Metropolitan centers of England and the continent, Ireland has been the subject of an enormous body of travel writing, especially by the English.[10] Travel writing in modern Europe has always provided its reading audiences with detailed ethnographic depictions of other ways of life. In both

10. For a useful bibliography of travel writing about Ireland see John McVeagh's *Irish Travel Writing: A Bibliography* (1996). McVeagh confirms the difficulty of identifying travel writing as a genre, because the lines between travel writing, literature, history, and anthropology are often blurry. About Irish travel writing, he writes, "This is such a various and shifting topic that no single definition of it would be likely to fit the topographical writings of so many different historical periods" (12). I think of early such early Irish novels as Maria Edgeworth's *The Absentee* (1812) and Lady Morgan's *Wild Irish Girl* (1806)as generically hybrid, in that large sections of these works read like travel narratives.

Ireland and across the globe, travel narratives, missionary chronicles, and colonial administrative reports were sources from which armchair comparative ethnologists such as James Frazer and E. B. Tylor synthesized massive amounts of information in producing such tome-like studies as, respectively, *The Golden Bough* and *Primitive Culture.* During the past three decades, as the discipline of anthropology has undergone a period of identity crisis and reassessment, scholars such as George Stocking and Mary Louise Pratt have turned to the history of the discipline, arguing that cultural anthropology stands in greater continuity with so-called unscientific travel writing than anthropologists of Bronislaw Malinowski's generation would allow.[11] James Buzard's work has been crucial in understanding how both popular and literary travel writing of the nineteenth century anticipated some of the key conventions of the formal academic anthropology of the twentieth century, "among them the achievement of ethnographic authority, the standpoint of 'participant observation,' the demarcation of distinct 'cultures,' and the relationship between a culture and its constituent 'details'" (1996, 167). Buzard also establishes the ways that nineteenth-century travel writing as undisciplined ethnography—or proto-ethnography—produced representations of cultures as self-contained and integrated wholes, in other words, modern "culture" as Malinowski would construct it in *Argonauts of the Western Pacific* (1922). He speculates that "the plural, holistic culture-concept is, if not the brainchild of an armchair comparativist, perhaps a close partner of that modern traveler's romance of perspective at once inside and outside of foreign life" (1996, 169).[12] Marc Manganaro argues that "culture" in its

11. Much of Malinowski's famous introduction to *Argonauts of the Western Pacific* concerns distinguishing the scientific methods of professional anthropologists from the untrained amateurism of nonprofessional travelers, missionaries, and so forth (1984, 1–25). He despised missionaries and thought their ethnographic writing to be of little value, even though he sometimes used it to orient his own study. As George Stocking shows, even much early academic ethnography of the late nineteenth century that grounded itself in fieldwork existed on the blurry line between amateur travel writing and academic anthropology (1992). For relevant discussions of anthropology's relation to travel see Buzard (1993a, 1996), Stocking (1992), and Pratt(1986).

12. See also Buzard's "A Continent of Pictures: Reflections on the 'Europe' of Nineteenth-Century Tourists" (1993b), in which he makes a similar argument.

modern form emerged through a cross-fertilization among disciplines, particularly literature and the social sciences. Reading the various permutations of "culture" in modernist texts situated around the year 1922, Manganaro makes a few significant claims about *Ulysses*: (1) that *Ulysses* is an ethnographic text in which Joyce, "like Malinowski, . . . works with words in the very terms of the 'things' those words attach, refer, or at least point toward" (2002, 113); (2) that Joyce, along with Malinowski and Eliot, constructs culture, "through the agency of the decline or collapse of that very process: Malinowski's Trobrianders, Eliot's Western Europeans, Joyce's Dubliners, all disappearing over the edge of the horizon of history and thus imperatively crying out for definition" (149–50). This conservative, or preservational, impulse in modernism, a staple of anthropology, is particularly apparent, as Gregory Castle reminds us, in Irish modernism, the product of uneven modernization (2001, 1–39). With Dublin no longer a plausible home for him, the city transformed after the Easter Rising, and a new Catholic Ireland emerging with the Free State, Joyce partakes in this preservational modernism, knowing that to preserve a cultural moment from the vantage point of almost two decades into the future is to have the freedom to project in fiction the lineaments of a new Ireland.

Likewise, if travel writing and other nondisciplinary proto-ethnographic writing can transmit a model of culture to the emerging discipline of ethnography, then it certainly must have done the same with the modern novel, as many novelists—Henry James, Joseph Conrad, and E. M. Forster, for instance—were prolific travel writers and readers. Joyce, who himself produced two thoughtful but conventional short travel pieces for the Triestine Irridentist periodical *Il Piccilo della Serra* in the late summer of 1912—"The City of Tribes" and "The Mirage of the Fishermen of Aran" (*CW*, 229–37)—was also an avid reader of travel writing, even reviewing a travel book, Harold Fielding Hall's *The Soul of the People,* in 1903 (*CW*, 93–95). Joyce's Triestine library, as cataloged by Michael Gillespie, contains eight clearly identifiable travel texts, both popular accounts such as Thomas Legh's *Narrative of a Journey in Egypt and the Country Beyond the Cataracts* as well as more literary books such as John Millington Synge's *Aran Islands,* and his letters give evidence of having read other travel narratives: those of Henry James and William Bulfin, for example (Mottolese 2002). Joyce's own perspective is shaped by travel, having detached himself from his tightly knit culture in Dublin and moved to Europe.

Ulysses should be read as a text of travel, as in its own way partaking in the travel writing tradition and as embodying what James Clifford calls "traveling culture," culture that takes shape not in rootedness but in and around travel, movement, and displacement (1997, 17–51). In Ireland's case, this is culture that moves through emigration, expatriation, or political transportation (i.e., diaspora) or as *Ulysses* depicts, culture that, as much as it is centered around the familiar social life of the rooted Catholic Northsiders,[13] encompasses all kinds of travelers: tourists, colonials, soldiers, sailors, imported commodities and ideas, operas, throwaways on the Liffey, and news about American maritime disasters and English horse races.

It is not surprising that Joyce weaves a self-described "Anglo-Saxon American['s]" narrative (Thompson 1893, 128) of travels across the globe into *Ulysses*. Nor is it surprising that Joyce depicts the well-read, liberal-minded Bloom, a fan of travel writing who has long fantasies in "Eumaeus" and "Ithaca" about traveling, as a character shaped by and oriented through the travel discourse of his time, as he himself travels through a culture that he lives within but, nonetheless, appears strange, even exotic, to him. The presence of *In the Track of the Sun* as a mental register for Bloom's ethnographic seeing draws attention not only to Bloom's ordinariness as a middle-class subject of the late Victorian British empire but also to Bloom's difference from others, or rather, of the difference of ordinary Dubliners from Bloom. As much as many Dubliners see him as foreign (a Jew), he is aware that their customs can be seen by an outsider as strange (remember Bloom's mantra in Burton's restaurant, "see ourselves as others see us" [8.662]). In a similar way, Thompson in *In the Track of the Sun* continually draws our attention to the strangeness of the cultures he observes: for instance, the near nakedness of children in Penang (90), Chinese foot binding (81–82), or Parsee funeral rituals (152).

Travel discourse frames and punctuates Leopold Bloom's day. Early in the morning when he first leaves his house, he thinks of *In the Track of the Sun*:

13. "Northsiders" is a term that James Fairhall uses to describe the same social group or culture that is central to the works of Joyce and Roddy Doyle (1993, 43–79).

"Travel round in front of the sun" (*U,* 4.84–85). He imagines a traveler—perhaps himself—in a "strange land" approaching a city: "walk along a strand, strange land, come to a city gate, sentry there, old ranker too" (*U,* 4.86–87). His mind then runs over scores of the "kind" (*U,* 4.99) of orientalist images that Thompson's book provides: "Old Tweedy's Big Moustaches, leaning on a kind of a long spear. Wander through awned streets, Turbaned faces going by. . . . Turko the terrible seated crosslegged, smoking a coiled pipe. Cries of sellers in the streets. Drink water scented with fennel, sherbet. . . . The shadows of mosques among pillars: priest with a scroll rolled up" (*U,* 4.87–93). In this early reflection, Bloom grasps some sense of the way orientalism, in Edward Said's formulation, works: the way images of the Asia and the Middle East have been exaggerated and exoticized within Western discourse. He finishes his musings accordingly: "Probably not a bit like it really. Kind of stuff you read: in the track of the sun" (*U,* 4.99–100). Bloom's day also concludes (at the end of "Ithaca") within the framework of travel. In "Ithaca" before Bloom falls asleep, he fantasizes about escaping his life and traveling through Ireland and the world (*U,* 17.1956–2008), and the episode ends with the words: "He rests. He has travelled" (*U,* 17.2320). As he falls asleep, he thinks of "Sinbad the Sailor," sounding variations of those words in his head in anapestic rhythm as he fades off (*U,* 17.2322–26).

Bloom has two notable lengthy fantasies about escape and travel late in *Ulysses,* one in "Ithaca" at the very end of the day and one in "Eumeaus," in which he drifts away from Murphy's yarn-spinning to daydream about a "longcherished plan he meant to one day realize . . . of travelling to London *via* long sea" (*U,* 16.499–502). In "Eumeaus," Bloom plots his course mostly through England but turns his reflections to travel and tourism in Ireland: "There were excellent opportunities for vacationists in the home island"(*U,* 16.547–548), and thinks about travel for its salubrious benefits, "for the chap whose liver [is] out of order" (*U,* 16.511) or for the individual looking for "rejuvenation" (*U,* 16.549) and a "bracing tonic" (*U,* 16.549–550). In "Ithaca," his fantasy of travel springs from a psychological need to escape his domestic condition of cuckoldry. He opts for "departure" over "decease" (*U,* 17.1956) as an escape and imagines a journey not just through some of the most famous tourist sites of Ireland—"the cliffs of Moher" to "the lakes of Killarney"—but around the globe, by way of many of the locations that

Thompson visits: Ceylon, Palestine, and the Bay of Naples among them (*U*, 17.1973–90). Bloom's wanderlust functions as a condition of his modernity or, more interestingly, his relative modernity in a largely traditional Dubliner culture. Born in 1866, Bloom grew up in an era of the secularization and democratization of travel (Duncan and Gregory 1999, 5–8), and he embodies what Dennis Porter calls the "curative dream of travel" (1993, 53), which he identifies as a symptom of modernity: "The faith that there are places on this earth where we may go in order to learn the secret of living freer, fuller, happier, more authentic or more purposeful lives than is currently the case where we happen to reside" (53). However, Bloom, rooted as he is within a traditional culture and bound by family ties, is going nowhere abroad, so he escapes into a fantasy world of travel, one which shapes his perceptions during his local peregrinations, and relativizes his perspective, allowing him to see his own people "as others see [them]" (*U*, 8.662) Daniel Lerner in *The Passing of Traditional Society* (1958), a study of a rapidly modernizing Middle East, identifies the "mobile personality," the modern individual in a traditional culture who, mostly through media and popular culture, gains an adaptability and "psychic mobility" (52) that enables one "to see oneself in the other fellows situation" (50). Such individuals can "see themselves as strange persons in strange situations, places, and time" (52). Bloom's own traveling imagination allows him to gain some of this modern "psychic mobility," a quality that his author also shares.

In the Track of the Sun is an extremely visual book. Thompson's globe-circling travels lead him from New York across the United States, through Japan, China, Ceylon, India, Persia, Egypt, Palestine, Turkey, and Europe, after which he takes a steamer from Liverpool, back home, "absent seven months and four days" (1893, 226). It contains seventy-nine full-page photographs and illustrations and about one small illustration per page. Thompson's tour is grand, and his book reveals a voyager who makes a great effort to claim the authority of a genuine "traveler," in the sense of James Buzard's "anti-tourist" (1993a). His book both aspires to a dizzying comparative comprehensiveness, moving quickly Westward across the entire globe "in front of the sun" (*U*, 4.84–85) and a localized holism, through which he tries to give the reader views of the many parts of single cultures. Thompson embodies Buzard's "romance of perspective, at once inside and outside of foreign life" (1996, 169). In China, he is a visitor, yet can take us into a typical Chinese home, gaze at the hairstyles of Chinese women, and speak with authority on Chinese foot-binding (1893, 80–82). As is true of many travel narratives—and less true of formal ethnography, which works to expunge and displace such elements—Thompson's gaze is voyeuristic, focusing frequently on women, often on their naked bodies. For example, in Japan, Thompson enters a bathhouse with a friend, where he watches "a dozen women . . . , all entirely nude" who "paid no attention" to them and "did not seem in the least degree disconcerted" (19). Bloom likely appreciated Thompson's fantasy of innocent eroticism, and his own Dublin voyaging fully shares in the voyeurism embedded in such orientalist travel accounts.[14]

Most striking in Thompson's travelogue are the illustrations and photographs, which are generally of two types: (1) scenic images, depicting landscapes, buildings, or ruins; (2) ethnographic photographs of natives in indigenous garb, engaging in putatively ordinary activities: sheiks on horses, snake-charmers, warriors with spears, and so forth. Though framed to appear natural, many of these ethnographic images are staged set pieces (some are retouched), in which the immobilized subjects gaze stolidly, or menacingly, at the camera, often with sets built around them (notice the floor, ersatz rocks, and theatrical backdrop in "A Turkish and an Egyptian Woman" [Figure 1]). In the pages of *In the Track of the Sun,* Bloom would have encountered numerous images in word, photo, or illustration that appear in some form in *Ulysses.* Not surprisingly, both Joyce and Bloom remember the visual images more than the words: the aforementioned shrouded Turkish and Egyptian women resemble the oriental Molly in the Eastern dreams of Stephen and Bloom. It is likely this image contributed to Joyce's description of the oriental Molly of "Circe": *"Beside her mirage of datepalms a handsome woman in Turkish costume stands before him. Opulent curves fill out her scarlet trousers and jacket, slashed with gold. A wide yellow cumberbund girdles her. A white yashmak, violet in the night, covers her face, leaving free only her large dark eyes and raven hair."* (*U,* 15.297–302, Joyce's italics).

14. Gregory Castle in *Modernism and the Celtic Revival* (2001) argues that Bloom practices an anthropological voyeurism. He reads this voyeurism as part of Joyce's critique of the anthropological practices of the Irish Revival.

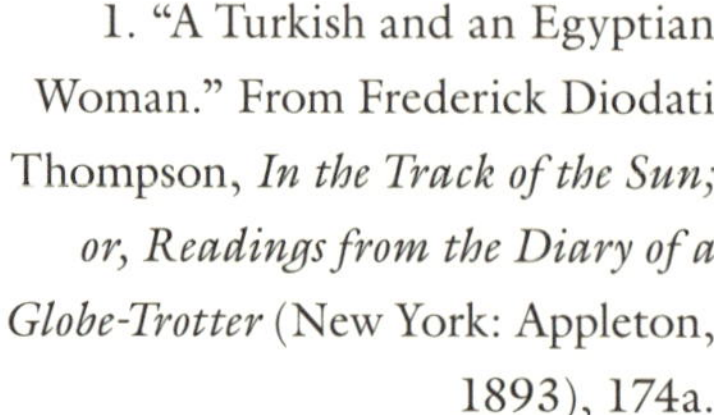

1. "A Turkish and an Egyptian Woman." From Frederick Diodati Thompson, *In the Track of the Sun; or, Readings from the Diary of a Globe-Trotter* (New York: Appleton, 1893), 174a.

2. "Kandian Chief, Ceylon." From Frederick Diodati Thompson, *In the Track of the Sun; or, Readings from the Diary of a Globe-Trotter* (New York: Appleton, 1893), 99.

3. "Bedouin Sheik from the Neighbourhood of Ghaza." From Frederick Diodati Thompson, *In the Track of the Sun; or, Readings from the Diary of a Globe-Trotter* (New York: Appleton, 1893), 164a.

4. "A Mohammedan Sheik." From Frederick Diodati Thompson, *In the Track of the Sun; or, Readings from the Diary of a Globe-Trotter* (New York: Appleton, 1893), 188a.

There are other such images in these early episodes that evoke photographs and illustrations in Thompson: "Cingalese lobbing about in the sun" (*U,* 5.32)—see Figure 2; a mustachioed Bedouin sheik on horseback leaning on a spear, just as Bloom imagines Major Tweedy (*U,* 4.87) and another sheik leaning on a pole—Figures 3 and 4; numerous mosques and bazaars and a "parsee tower." (*U,* 6.987) With accuracy, Gifford and Seidman trace this image back to page 156 of *In the Track of the Sun,* on which there is a photograph of vultures perching on a stunted circular tower (Gifford and Seidman 1988, 125).

While Bloom thinks of *In the Track of the Sun* as late as "Nausicaa" (*U,* 13.805), and a good part of "Eumaeus" consists of the fantastical travel stories of Murphy the sailor, his mind travels most in the early episodes as he makes his way from his neighborhood toward the city's center. In these same episodes, especially in "Calypso," "Lotus-Eaters," and "Hades," Joyce uses Bloom most consistently to show the reader Dublin life. James Boon says of anthropology: "The purpose of anthropology is to make superficially exotic practices appear familiar and superficially familiar practices appear exotic" (1983, 132). Boon's definition would suggest that Bloom sees the world anthropologically, as Gregory Castle has recently argued, characterizing Bloom's voyeuristic gaze as destabilizing any anthropological certainty (Castle 2001, 208–47). Throughout the early part of his journey, Bloom's anthropological observations of Dublin entwine with his thoughts about places far and wide, as he shuttles between observing Dublin and thinking about foreign places. For example, in "Calypso" while alone in the heart of the north inner city, Bloom thinks of Gibraltar (*U,* 4.60, 4.112), Bulgaria (*U,* 4.63), Russia (*U,* 4.116), Japan (*U,* 4.117), Turkey (*U,* 4.192), Palestine ("Agendath Netaim") (*U,* 4.191–97, 219–28), Germany (*U,* 4.199), Spain (*U,* 4.211), "The Levant" (*U,* 4.212), Norway (*U,* 4.215), Greece (*U,* 4.372–77), and England (*U,* 4.503). The succeeding episodes continue this pattern. Bloom adds to the atlas of his thoughts: Ceylon (*U,* 5.29–36), Austria (*U,* 5.199), "Eldorado" (*U,* 5.215), St. Peter Clavier and Africa (*U,* 5.323), China (*U,* 5.326–28)—he even recalls Viator's *Voyages in China* (one of the books in his library [*U,* 6.983–84])—America (*U,* 5.547), "fleshpots of Egypt" (*U,* 5.548), "Hindu widows" in India (*U,* 6.548), Rome (*U,* 6.644), and the "parsee tower" of Persia (*U,* 6.997). In many cases, as I have suggested, Bloom accompanies his thoughts of exotic places with amusing, often spurious ethnographic observations: "I read that in *Voyages in China* that the Chinese say a white man smells like a corpse" (*U,* 114). What Bloom sees and thinks about most often, however, is Dublin life: both a largely moribund Dubliner culture, and a more diverse port city.

The travel discourse that fills Bloom's consciousness shapes his images of the world. Its ubiquity suggests that Bloom sees and thinks about both the world and his own community as a traveler and outsider might. Bloom brings the exotic into the familiar world of Dublin while simultaneously making the Dubliners appear exotic. In fact, Bloom often produces anthropological observations about Dublin that are as outrageous as his thoughts about foreign cultures and as dubious as many of the images of *In the Track of the Sun*. We see a number of these moments in "Lotus-Eaters." During his visit to All Hallows Church, he concludes that I.N.R.I. stands for "Iron nails ran in" (*U,* 5.374) and even hypothesizes that the priest uses wine in the Eucharistic ceremony because wine "makes it more aristocratic than for example if he drank what they are used to Guinness's porter or some temperance beverage" (*U,* 5.387–88). At the same time, the scene has a soporific and narcotic atmosphere of the kind Thompson found in the tropics. Similarly, the Eucharistic ritual that he witnesses is quite strange to him. Bloom defamiliarizes the Catholic Eucharistic ceremony by comparing it to cannibalism, "Rum idea: eating bits of corpse" (*U,* 5.352), and speculates that it has a narcotic but unifying effect on the communicants: "Now I bet it makes them feel happy. Lollipop. . . . Then they all feel like one family party, same in the theatre, all in the same swim. . . . Not so lonely. . . . Old fellow asleep near that confessional box. Hence those snores. Blind Faith, Safe in the arms if kingdom come. Lulls all pain" (*U,* 5.359–68). Upon entering the church, Bloom sees a note for Fr. Conmee's speech on Saint Peter Claver, and he thinks of Africans and then the Chinese, "prefer an ounce of opium. Celestials. Rank heresy for them. Buddha their god lying on his side in the museum. Taking it easy with hand under his cheek. Jossticks burning" (*U,* 5.327–29). While Thompson does not mention opium use, his book is full of images of and references to Buddha, including a magnificent photograph of the Great Buddha as a frontispiece. But Bloom is as misinformed about Chinese religion (Buddha is not "their god") as he is about Irish religion, though appreciative of and curious about both. This scene as much suggests Bloom's distance from this common Dublin ritual as it objectifies the ritual as an ethnographically significant act worthy of observation and interpretation. The narrator of "Ithaca" describes one of Bloom's "intellectual pursuits" as the "comparative study of religion" (*U,* 17.1588–89). Thus, the juxtaposition of the Roman Catholic Eucharistic ceremony with Chinese opium eaters and Buddha suggests Bloom's comparative anthropological mentality. The Dubliners have their own traditions, but these traditions take their place in a much larger world of cultural phenomena. Likewise, Joyce suggests, these traditions have been as often misunderstood and misrepresented by outsiders as those of the Chinese.

In "Hades," Bloom partakes in a funeral ritual that he finds impractical and hard to understand. As in "Lotus Eaters," he interpolates ethnographic observations about exotic cultures with those about Dubliners. Although he not only participates in and carefully observes the many rituals involved in Paddy Dignam's funeral, he makes occasional and comic stabs at explaining them. About a Latin blessing, he thinks, "Makes them feel more important to be prayed over in Latin" (*U,* 6.602). Moments later, Bloom sees the priest take "a stick with a knob at the end of it out of [a] bucket and [shake] it over the coffin" (*U,* 6.614–15). This act of sprinkling holy water, a common ritual in Catholic Ireland, becomes for Bloom an odd and awkward gesture. Joyce's language is defamiliarizing: Bloom sees a "knob" and "bucket" and does not seem sure what is happening, but he explains it away, nonetheless: "It's all written down: he has to do it" (*U,* 6.617). In the same scene, Bloom thinks of Hindu women immolating themselves (*U,* 6.548), "whores in turkish graveyards" (*U,* 6.757), "Chinese cemetaries with giant poppies [that] produce the best opium" (*U,* 6.769–70), the Chinese view that "a white man smells like a corpse" (U 6.983) and the "parsee tower of silence" (*U,* 6.987). Interestingly, Bloom's language as he thinks about the Parsee tower—"Ashes to ashes. Or bury at sea. Where is the Parsee tower? Eaten by birds" (*U,* 6.986–87)—evokes not only Thompson's photograph of the tower but also his description of the Parsee funeral ritual in India: "Perched on the top of the tower are usually a number of vultures waiting for the approach of the funeral. The procession stops near the tower. Only the bearers of the corpse enter with the body and lay it, with all its clothing removed, on the tower's top. On their retirement the vultures descend, leaving only bones, which are thrown into a central pit of the tower, to resolve themselves into dust and ashes" (1893, 155). Bloom's "mobile personality," shaped by his exposure through reading travel writing to many parts of the globe, so often takes him far from static Dublin. He cannot help but stand a little outside its curious social life.

Among the close-knit group of Dublin men participating in Paddy Dignam's funeral, Bloom travels mostly around the margins as an internal deviant or outsider. At times, it must be noted, he functions comfortably as an insider. For example, two of his earliest street encounters reveal Bloom as a familiar member of the culture, at least when his fellow Dubliners are soliciting a favor from him. With M'Coy in "Calypso," Bloom brooks annoying small talk and gossip and carries M'Coy's tidings to Dignam's funeral. His ensuing encounter with Bantam Lyons is also friendly and familiar: "Hello Bloom. What's the best news?" (*U,* 5.520). Lyons even perceives Bloom as a source of gambling tips, as if he were a regular among the pub-going crowd. More often, Bloom is cast as a oddball and outsider, as in "Cyclops." Most typically, however, the traveler Bloom flits furtively on the fringes of Dubliner culture, himself different from the cultural norm but at the same time an emblem of Joyce's cultural assessment and projection in *Ulysses*: caught between tradition and modernity but an avatar of a more vigorous, worldly, and kinetic Ireland to come.

Although Gregory Castle in *Modernism and the Celtic Revivial* is right to a degree that Bloom's voyeurism represents Joyce's critique of anthropology, this voyeurism is itself a major feature of the ethnography of travel, and it figures largely in *In the Track of the Sun.* Many have argued that Bronislaw Malinowski had to displace his voyeuristic fantasies to his diaries, as such fantasies would have invalidated his scientific ethnography. But the content of Bloom's thought is more the ethnography of travel than social science, so his voyeurism might be termed conventional for its genre, if a bit extreme at times. Joyce, rather, launches his most trenchant critiques of anthropology in the experimental later episodes. "Eumaeus," for example, questions whether fact or truth can ever be communicated accurately. Embedded in the center of this episode of uncertainties, misperceptions, and half-truths are the exotic travel narratives and yarns of Murphy, the Irish English sailor. Murphy's stories exemplify the tendency of travel writing to romanticize and embellish knowledge about other peoples. Even the photograph that he flourishes of "a group of savage women striped in loincloth, squatted, blinking, suckling, frowning, sleeping amid of swarm of infants . . . outside some primitive shanties of oiser" (*U,* 16.475–78) frames an exoticized and primitived image for the eyes of Western Europeans, much as Thompson's book does (and in this case, the kind of swarming squalor that had too often been used to demean the Catholic Irish).[15]

To read *Ulysses* in the track of Leopold Bloom means seeing a studied reality already mediated by travel discourse, already tinted by images from the travel narratives Bloom (and Joyce) had read. In this way, Joyce reminds us of the difficulty of seeing culture in any clear or stable way and of the futility of representing it accurately. However, when it comes to the Irish, Bloom, the conventional traveler, though at times critical, rarely, if ever, embraces the Manicheanism of primitive and civilized that undergirds nineteenth-century travel writing. Although he has the psychic mobility to see the oddness, ugliness, and paralysis that Dubliners frequently manifest, he is not an imperial man who derogates, primitivizes, and infantalizes the Irish, the nationality he claims as his own. While he finds their eating habits dirty in "Lestrygonians" and the political views of their extremists unpalatable in "Cyclops," Bloom lives his life with respect, good will, and patience—even taking seriously a debate with the bellicose Citizen. *Ulysses,* especially in the early episodes with their dense depictions of Dublin life, might best be described as autoethnographic: a term denoting the representation of a culture by one of its own members. Admittedly, Joyce questions and critiques anthropological conventions in *Ulysses,* most trenchantly in the novel's later episodes (e.g., "Eumeaus"), but an ethnographically realistic mode characterizes much of the novel's style. Moreover, that this representation is autoethnographic—self-ethnographic—gives *Ulysses* a better *claim* to authenticity than Haines's book could ever have, even if that representa-

15. Bloom's own anthropological observations about Molly and the "Spanish Type" as having "passionate termperments" in "Eumaeus" are as spurious as Murphy's stories (*U,* 16.873–90).

tion is shaped by colonialist terms. Trying to attach word to thing, Joyce constructs a recognizable culture in *Ulysses* that remains an important part of the novel, even as he simultaneously confirms the futility and, in the case of most ethnography, the discursive violence of doing so. Bloom's view of Dublin may not be objective or authentic, but Joyce created a character with a mind worldly enough and a local knowledge deep enough to help us see Dublin as others see it.

6

What's Wrong with Hybridity

The Impotence of Postmodern Political Ideals in *Ulysses* and *Midnight's Children*

MICHAEL TRATNER

IN POSTCOLONIAL THEORY, hybridity has replaced older political ideals that were often invoked during the decades of colonial liberation, in particular nationalism and Marxism. Those older ideals have become tainted with imposing new forms of oppression after the end of colonialism, due to what David Lloyd has called their "monologic desire"—their wish to create a kind of unified social order which has the effect of suppressing groups within the new postcolonial society (Lloyd 1993, 89). Hybridity seeks to maintain differences, whereas nationalism and Marxism seek to eliminate certain differences: nationalism dreams of removing all traces of the colonial influence; Marxism dreams of removing the ruling class. The "monologic desire" of each of these movements casts some part of the social order into the role of pure "oppressor," an "other" that can only be excised through revolution, not hybridized. Hence, these earlier movements also accept and advocate violence, the forced removal of wealth or even the bodies of those evil segments of the social order. Hybridity postulates instead a transformation of both oppressive and oppressed portions of the social order, dreaming of mixing identities so completely that no one would ever conceive of oppressing some "other" because there simply wouldn't be any identifiable "other."

But in advocating mergers and mixings rather than forcible changes in status of social groups, hybridity theory can end up almost completely without force of any sort—in other words, impotent, except as a vaguely utopian ideal devoid of any praxis for making it real. This problem with hybridity permeates two of the postcolonial novels most often praised for their visions of hybridity as a political ideal: Joyce's *Ulysses* and Rushdie's *Midnight's Children*. Each of these novels stages the confrontation between hybrid and monological thinking as a confrontation of allegorized characters. In *Ulysses* we have Bloom, the embodiment of multiplicity—Jew/Irish/Hungarian—confronting the Citizen, embodiment of Cyclopian single-mindendness. In *Midnight's Children,* we similarly have the confrontation of Saleem, the advocate of peaceful telepathic hybridity, and Shiva, the advocate of a war to decide a single ruling gang. In each novel, the reader is unquestionably placed on the side of the advocates of hybridity: for all of Bloom's silliness and stupidity, his basic humanity triumphs over the prejudicial judgment of the Citizen; and for all of Saleem's self-doubts, he remains the moral voice of the novel, even when condemning himself. A number of critics who treat Joyce and Rushdie as postcolonial authors have developed much more complex versions of such arguments: Vincent Cheng and Enda Duffy have traced in great detail Joyce's "sensitivity towards the nature of . . . hybridity"; Shailja Sharma argues that "Rushdie's freewheeling use of hybridity . . . gives his work its iconoclastic, transgressive edge" and suggests that Rushdie and Joyce belong together as authors who have made hybridity "a determining feature of counterhegemonic literature and politics" (Cheng 1995, 56; Duffy 1994; Sharma 2001, 603, 596). Rushdie himself describes his novels as celebrating "hybridity, impurity, intermingling, the transformation that comes of new and unexpected combinations of human beings, cultures, ideas, politics, movies, songs" (Rushdie 1992, 394); Joyce and Rushdie seem then to join with theorists such as Homi Bhaba and Gloria Anzaldúa in the postmodern rejection of all the "isms"—sexism, racism, nationalism, statism, ethnocentrism, and even Marxism—which become rather similar to each other in their single-mindedness (Bhabha 1983b; Anzaldúa 1999).

However, interpretations of *Ulysses* and *Midnight's Children* as advocating hybridity stumble upon the detail I mentioned earlier: the nagging association in these novels between hybridity and impotence. Bloom and Saleem, the allegorical representations of hybridity, are to some degree impotent sexually and decidedly impotent politically: they talk about sexual and political dreams, but they cannot fulfill their desires, so both novels end with a degree of sadness at personal and social failure. Of course, there are various ways to interpret the theme of impotence while preserving the value of the hybridity represented in the novel. One can claim that the characters are only partially allegorical, or one can claim that impotence represents the external oppression imposed upon the characters and upon the politics of hybridity. *Midnight's Children* ends by suggesting that oppressive forces bring about Saleem's impotence and the failure of the "political" party he founded: he is castrated and the members of the Midnight's Children Conference are hunted down by Indira Gandhi's forces. And Bloom's impotence could be interpreted as a result of the prejudice he meets everywhere: Joyce suggests such an interpretation by revealing that deep in Bloom's unconscious (as revealed in "Circe") his sexuality has become a masochistic desire for degradation; in other words, his sex life has been warped by internalized oppression. One could then conclude that the impotence of these characters and the analogous failure of their dreams of hybridity to become political reality are due to the insidious power of monological thinking, which somehow survives the transformation from colony to postcolonial nation.

However, the associations between impotence and hybridity are simply too strong in these novels to dismiss entirely as a result of external oppression. Rushdie in particular will not allow readers to escape the implications of Saleem's impotence so easily: the novel states repeatedly that Saleem's failure to achieve any of his desires, sexual or political, derives from deep flaws in his own character, long before he is castrated and long before the members of his movement are hunted down. The book further strongly implies that these flaws in Saleem allegorically represent flaws in hybridity itself. *Midnight's Children* thus contains a deep critique of hybridity along with its obvious advocacy of it, and exploring this critique can reveal similar trends in Joyce's novel, suggesting we have to read both these books in a rather less progressive light than critics such as Cheng, Duffy, and Sharma have presented.

Rushdie is quite explicit about giving an allegorical political reading of Saleem's impotence, by interpreting the cause of that impotence: an "unnatural" lust for his sister. This lust arises only when his sister is transformed from The Brass Monkey into Jamila Singer, a transformation that makes her essentially the voice of antihybridity, "dedicated . . . to patriotism . . . faith-in-leaders and trust-in-God," her "voice . . . a sword for purity" (1991,

376–77). It is precisely the monological character of her singing that inspires Saleem's lust, as he explains himself: "Is it possible to trace the origins of unnatural love? Did Saleem, who had yearned after a place in the centre of history, become besotted with what he saw in his sister of his own hopes for life? Did [he] fall in love with the new wholeness of his sibling?" (380). The unnaturalness of his love is then not simply that it conflicts with nature in general, but that it conflicts with his particular "nature," with everything he seemed elsewhere in the book to represent: nonwholeness, noncentrality, or, in other words, hybridity. And because he feels this love to be unnatural, it does not lead to his devotion to purity and wholeness; on the contrary, he is simply paralyzed by his lust for wholeness, and devotes himself instead to its opposite: "The sacred, or good, held little interest for me, even when such aromas surrounded my sister as she sang; while the pungency of the gutter seemed to possess a fatally irresistible attraction" (381). His fatally irresistible attraction to the gutter becomes as devoid of any possibility of achieving any satisfaction as his lust for Jamila: he goes into the gutter and remains impotent for the rest of his life. Rushdie is suggesting that hybridity lusts after hegemonic power and unity, so that even when it seems to be celebrating the marginal and gutter parts of society (as both Rushdie's and Joyce's novel do), it is really dreaming of the center. These novel may be, like Saleem, exploring the gutter as a way of keeping themselves from giving in to their deep desire for centrality, purity and power, a desire which feels "unnatural."

It might seem that I am reading quite a bit into the brief description of Saleem's unnatural lust, but the view that hybridity is rendered impotent by its secret desire for centrality, unity, and nonhybridity is repeated in two other places in the novel, and in those places it appears directly as a political theme, as an explanation of the failure of Saleem's "dream for India." Saleem's political dream is of finding a way to bring all the different groups in India to have a deep understanding of each other. He has a magical gift to bring this dream into reality: through him, all the "midnight's children," who seem to represent all the varied populaces within India, can communicate telepathically with each other. This collection of disparate persons able to be mentally in tune with each other becomes then an image of the ideal governing body of a hybrid nation, and Saleem gives it a political name: he calls it the Midnight's Children Conference (MCC)and tries to shape it as what he calls a "loose federation of equals, all points of view given free expression" (263). Shiva, the embodiment of monological desire, responds that such a view is nonsense, because "Gangs gotta have gang bosses" (263).

Eventually, Shiva leaves the Midnight Children's Conference and joins a different "party" with a very definite boss—Indira Gandhi—which then takes as one of its prime goals the complete destruction of the Midnight's Children Conference. But that physical destruction is an anticlimax; the failure of the conference occurs much earlier and is attributed by the novel to a flaw in Saleem—another illicit desire like his lust for Jamila's wholeness and centrality. The desire this time is for wealth, the wealth he had growing up, which he discovers he received only accidentally and in some sense unfairly as a result of a switch at birth involving him and Shiva. A woman inspired by communist rhetoric switches the baby of poor parents (Saleem) and the one of rich parents (Shiva) so that Saleem is raised by the rich and Shiva by the poor. Saleem learns of this but refuses to let Shiva or any of the Midnight's Children know, for fear that Shiva would take away Saleem's place in the wealthy family. The failure of the Midnight's Children Conference is presented as directly caused by Saleem's unwillingness to reveal this fact. To avoid revealing it, he has to block off part of his mind whenever he convenes the conference, and the other Midnight's Children become aware of his blockage and attack him for it. It is this attack that is credited with destroying the Conference:

> The children of midnight . . . attacked on a broad front and from every direction, accusing me of secrecy, prevarication, high-handedness, egotism; my mind, no longer a parliament chamber, became the battleground on which they annihilated me . . . I listened helplessly while they tore me apart; because, despite all their sound-and-fury, I could not unblock what I had sealed away: I could not bring myself to tell them Mary's secret . . . now, as the midnight's children lost faith in me, they also lost their belief in the thing I had made for them. (358)

The conference loses its idealistic political form—it no longer is a "parliament chamber" because its founder refuses to share with the others, refuses equality. When the Children lose their "belief" in what Saleem had "made," the Conference is "destroyed by things—bickerings, prejudices, boredom, selfishness—which I had believed too small, too petty to have touched them" (358). In other words, the power of prejudice and selfishness, those prime opponents of hybridity, only win out over multicultural understanding because of a kind of corruption within the one person with the power to create that multicultural understanding. The dream of hybridity dies because Saleem is unwilling to accept a loss of wealth as its cost.

By presenting Saleem and Shiva as babies switched at birth, Rushdie suggests some very disturbing notions about hybridity. Saleem's and Shiva's opposed political theories may be the result, then, of the status of their upbringings. In other words, hybridity may derive from the elite position of its advocates, while single-minded desire for power and wealth may derive from the deprivations of unfair poverty. The distinction between the two may not be a distinction between understanding and blind narrow-mindedness; there may be material causes of these opposed "faiths" and it may require material change (a real cost) for the advocates of hybridity to bring about what they want. Hybridity is not simply divorced from material social structures such as wealth and poverty; rather, it is a product of such structures and rendered impotent as a political movement by its unwillingness to recognize that fact.

When Rushdie presents the destruction of the Midnight's Children Conference due to Saleem's refusal to admit his entwinement with Shiva, there is another allegorical element swirled into the mix, one that brings this story closer to the tale of Saleem's lust for Jamila. As in that story, there is a desire for national glory that also contributes to the failure of the dream of they hybrid nation. Rushdie brings in the role of national glory by staging the moment when the children attack Saleem as coincident with China's war with India and interleaving news reports about the war and descriptions of the Children's war on Saleem. Thus, the scene begins: "UNPROVOKED ATTACK ON INDIA—the questions I'd been dreading and trying not to provoke began: *Why is Shiva not here? And Why have you closed off part of your mind?*" (357). And as India loses the war, the text reads "Gurkhas and Rajputs fled in disarray from the Chinese army; and in the upper reaches of my mind, another army was also destroyed, by prejudice and selfishness" (358). So the destruction of the hybridity movement parallels rather strangely India's loss in this war. Rushdie provides an interpretation of the connection between the two by paralleling two different kinds of "drainage." When India loses the war, a headline declares, "PUBLIC MORALE DRAINS AWAY." Immediately after that, Saleem is "drained" by doctors hired by his parents, his nose cleared by an operation that removes his telepathic powers, and that seals the destruction of the Midnight's Children Conference. By paralleling the collapse of the belief in India's glory and the collapse of the Midnight's Children's Conference, Rushdie suggests the disturbing thought that the willingness to accept differences in a hybrid social order may depend on an underlying sense of national glory and wholeness. The logic of such a connection is not hard to see: when people feel that the nation is strong and whole, differences among them do not seem so great that they threaten to tear apart the social fabric. Prejudice and selfishness can then be overcome by a hybrid "loose federation" only when there is a deep belief in the glory of the nation to unite the differing groups. In other words, the parallel to the war with China suggests as does the tale of Saleem's lust for Jamila that hybridity depends on an "unnatural" connection to its opposite, to nationalism and chauvinism. Just as Saleem is rendered sexually impotent by his lusting after his sister's wholeness, his movement is rendered politically impotent by its dependence on a sense of national glory that it would seem to overtly oppose.

There is one more moment when Saleem gives an account of why his dream of changing India failed, and his account in this case is slightly different, but once again there is an attitude inside Saleem that is presented as the cause of the failure of his political dream. The moment occurs when Saleem meets what he calls "the greatest man I ever met," Picture Singh, who advocates a "socialism which owed nothing to foreign influences" and promotes his socialism by staging snake-dances that allegorically comment on the social order (474, 476). Saleem reacts by saying:

> Something in me objected to Picture's portrayal in snake-dance of the unrelieved vileness of the rich; I found myself thinking, "There is good and bad in all—and they brought me up, they look after me, Pictureji!" After which I began to see . . . in fact, my dream of saving the country was a thing of mirrors and smoke; insubstantial, the maunderings of a fool. (493)

It seems on one level that this case is similar to the others: Saleem has a private "desire"—his love for his childhood family—that gets in the way of his political dream; if he would have to declare the wealthy people who raised him were "vile" in order to create equality, he would not do it. However, there is something more here than merely Saleem's private desires getting in the way of his general politics: the text brings forth an essential piece of the logic of hybridity itself as causing Saleem's dream to be impossible. When Saleem says that "there is good and bad in all," he is saying that he wants to preserve and bring together all groups within society, not eliminate any as Singh would. And somehow, this very ideal of preserving all differences proves to Saleem that his dream of saving the country is an illusion.

The essential logic of hybridity is at stake here: hybridity theory depends on the notion that there is "good and bad in all" and seeks to preserve the good in all groups by hybridizing them together. The problem this scene highlights is that hybridity theory refuses to consider the necessity of eliminating some social group or destroying its status as part of the process of creating the political dream of a hybrid nation. Revolutionary theory like Marx's depends instead on the basic tenet that some differences must be eliminated—differences of class. Marxist theory rejects the notion that all social groups can coexist peacefully, because what is inside each class (call it consciousness or ideology or just values) implies the suppression of what is inside other classes. Those who view classes in terms of such conflicts tend to treat the "difference" between the mentalities of the two classes in terms of true and false beliefs. Marx labels the mentality of the upper class "false consciousness" and calls for revolution to expose it as illusory; those in the upper class label the mentality of the lower class "ignorance" and call either for laws to keep it from having influence or education to eliminate it. The two opposed classes end up agreeing that ultimately the goal is to have only one class left: either the upper is all that will be expressed and visible (through oppression or education) or the lower will become the only one (through revolution).

Saleem rejects that model and substitutes the notion that different groups, such as the rich and the poor, are simply "different," not truer or falser than each other. This substitution of the logic of difference for the logic of class is not just Saleem's private theory: it is a project that was carried out extensively in the twentieth century as a way of resisting Marxism. Class was redefined as one of many "differences," joining race, ethnicity, religion, and gender in making up a patchwork society. Once class is understood that way, then eliminating any class, such as the "vile rich," becomes as unthinkable as genocide. Our understanding of class structure has been transformed into a part of a dominant model of hybridity in twentieth century news reporting and social theory. I am not talking about some postmodern intellectual concept when I speak of such a dominant model of hybridity; I am just referring to what has become a regular part of social analysis in newspapers, namely "demographics." Every election is analyzed in terms of the voting pattern of a whole range of subcultures, and economic "classes" are simply a subset. Often demographic analyses break up the social order into as many as ten different "classes" or income groups. Demographic analyses treat such "classes" as things ontologically identical to racial, gender, religious, and ethnic groups—all of them produce "differences" in thought and voting patterns, contributing to the wonderful mixture of the country. To want fewer people in the bottom income categories—in other words, to want to reduce poverty—becomes in a bizarre way similar to wanting to eliminate some races from the mix. So does wanting to shrink the top income categories to reduce inequality. As Saleem puts it, "There is good and bad in all."

Putting all three of these moments of explanation of the impotence of Saleem's political dreams and of his body, Rushdie presents a powerful critique of hybridity: it is, this novel implies, a theory devoid of material force in several senses. Hybridity refuses to use the weapons of power (i.e., violence); it refuses to remove material wealth from anyone to achieve equality; it refuses to accept the elimination of differences even if they are unfair; it is torn by a hidden desire for centrality and wholeness; it may be a product of the material wealth of its advocates; and it depends on a sense of national glory to reduce the splintering effect of differences. In other words, hybridity lusts secretly after power and wealth and inequality, after all those qualities to which is its publically opposed—and thus renders itself impotent.

Rushdie also implies the converse conclusion, that monological thinking is quite potent: Shiva not only fathers numerous children, he fathers Saleem's own child, in whom Saleem puts his faith for a better political result than his own efforts produced. Potency ultimately refers to the power to create something new, and the novel suggests in is representation of Shiva that destruction is necessary for any real creation. To create a child, a nation, a culture, something has to be destroyed, eliminated, and not merely hybridly preserved (or pickled, to use Saleem's fond metaphor).

Hybridity, seeking only to understand its opponents, not to destroy them, cannot ultimately create a new future: it really only acts mentally, not physically or materially. Rushdie discusses the difference between acts that involve material change and those that involve merely mental images in his discussion of different ways that the world of Saleem interacts with the larger world of Indian politics. He presents four different modes of what he calls "connection" between a person's life and history. The four derive from two poles: active/passive (does Saleem cause events in the larger world or merely get pushed around by them?) and literal/metaphorical (do the events in Saleem's world and in the larger world physically affect each other, or do they merely metaphorically mirror each other?). After explaining examples of how Saleem's life and India's history have all four connections, he goes on to say that the Midnight's Children Conference operated in only three of the four modes, only in the "passive-metaphorical, passive-literal, and active-metaphorical . . . but it never became what I most wanted it to be; we never operated in the first, most significant of the 'modes of connection.' The "active-literal" passed us by" (286). In other words, the political organization devoted to the creation of a hybrid nation fails to become a material agent in history. Its only agency, its only form of "active" connection to history, is "metaphorical"—it can create images of he complexity of the nation, but it does not alter that complexity. The Children would seem to have great power—each has a magical ability—but the book suggests that magic is precisely a metaphor of power, not really a version of power: magic in this book does not actually accomplish anything. Hybridity is a kind of magical action upon the state, seeking effects through the operation of "culture," not through material means such as economics or violence.

Joyce's novel *Ulysses* is entirely structured on passive or metaphoric methods of "connecting" to history. As its title suggests, whatever commentary it has to make on the twentieth century world will be presented through analogies and parallels. The novel clearly connects with the issues of burning importance during Ireland's transformation from a colony to a partitioned pair of modern states, but it addresses those issues almost entirely through analogy, never through direct (i.e., material) analysis. For example, instead of examining the way that Catholic Ireland sought to emerge from its oppressed position within the Protestant British empire, Joyce presents a parallel: he traces the efforts of a Jew of Hungarian ancestry to emerge from an oppressed position within the Irish Catholic community. By focusing on this ethnic conflict instead of the ones at the center of political struggles in Ireland in 1904, questions of economic and political power disappear, replaced by general questions about the nature of prejudice. The biggest moment of political confrontation in the novel—Bloom facing the Citizen—is devoid of the political and economic structures that would surround a confrontation of an Irish Catholic and British Protestant leader: the Citizen has no official political power over Bloom and even seems to have less money than Bloom. Bloom's inclusive and nonviolent answer to the verbal violence directed at him —saying "Your God was a jew" (*U,* 342 l.30; 12.1808) is roughly the same as Saleem's statement, "There is good and bad in all." As the citizen tries to condemn Jews to the category of purely worthless "other," Bloom claims that what the Citizen regards as central to his own group—God—is already Jewish, so there is no way to excise Jewishness from Christian society.

Bloom attempts to undermine the intellectual basis of the Citizen's attitudes, but says nothing about changing the structures of power and wealth that surround the Citizen and Bloom. Intellectual and emotional changes seem sufficient because the threat to Bloom is represented as entirely intellectual and emotional—an attitude—not backed up by any form of power. There is of course a representation of the Citizen trying to use power to enforce his attitude: he hurls a biscuit tin at Bloom. If we were to interpret the biscuit tin as a symbolic representation of the violence used to maintain oppressive ethnic systems, we would be forced to conclude that such violence is easy to avoid and of little consequence.

There is a confrontation later in the book that would seem to show more directly colonial violence, a physical "fight" between an Irish Catholic and some British Protestants: Stephen's confrontation with British sailors, which ends with their knocking him out. But the violence that ends the scene seems a result of inability to understand intelligent speech rather than anything that has to do with competing claims on political power. Note that Stephens' speech to the British sailors, like Saleem's answer to Picture Sing and Bloom's answer to the Citizen, refuses to pick sides in a conflict. Stephen claims to be part of no nation and no religion, to be a marginalized person disconnected from any social movement. Hybridity theory seeks to bring everyone to a position something like Stephen's, to see themselves as not fully inside any single group, and so marginal to every group. Stephen may carry the view too far, into a version of nihilism, but it is simply a variant of the view that no group can be preferred to any other—and, like Bloom's and Saleem's views, it is useless as the basis of any political movement. Stephen's refusal to honor the British king, like Bloom's resistance to the Citizen's rhetoric, comes as part of no economic or political movement.

Stephen does end up knocked out, so the violence directed against his speech is rather more effective than that directed against Bloom. Given that this violence is meted out by members of the colonizing army, we could read the end of this scene as showing that intellectual freedom is not enough, that some answer to institutionalized violence is necessary. The novel does not lead in any such direction: indeed, it undermines any impulse a reader might have to slug the sailors back: that would just reduce the reader to the level of the stupid idiots who misunderstood Stephen. Putting this scene together with Bloom's confrontation with the Citizen, we can conclude that this book shows that on both sides of the Irish troubles—among the British and as among the Irish nationalists—persons who use violence to achieve their ends are stupid and misdirect that power. So the conflicts tearing Ireland apart end up seeming due to the stupidity of the leaders of all movements, their inability to transcend mistaken visions, their prejudicial blindness. Prejudice is not presented as having any relationship to maintaining or gaining wealth or power. So instead of advocating economic change or violence, this novel offers intellectual freedom, a form of hybridity liberated from all economic and political forces. As such its hybridity is entirely mental or aesthetic, not political.

The two scenes of direct confrontation epitomize what goes on throughout the novel. In numerous ways, *Ulysses* transforms the postcolonial politics of conflicting group interests into a purely intellectual contest that eviscerates the need for changes in structures of power or wealth. The transformation of conflicting group interests into purely intellectual differences structures the central "plot" of the book—the bringing together Stephen and Bloom, two persons defined as culturally different. The interaction of Stephen and Bloom enacts the crucial goal of hybridity theory: bringing two parts of one nation to recognize their differences, accept them simply as differences, and mix them together until there is no longer a possibility of one part oppressing the other. The end of Stephen's and Bloom's encounter, chapter 17, is basically a long list of "differences" that are often mixed together in amusing ways.

What Joyce does not consider at all is that there are material differences between the two "cultures" that Bloom and Stephen represent. The easiest way to see this material difference is to consider how the two men have different amounts of "cultural capital" as we can see through their different educations. Stephen is university educated, and Bloom ended his education at high school. The main conclusion the book presses us toward is that the two different educations are just that: different, neither better nor worse. Both Bloom and Stephen are clearly quite smart, quite thoughtful, quite "interesting" to us as readers, though most readers probably feel relatively better educated than Bloom and worse educated than Stephen. What is most important, though, is that Stephen is not represented as gaining any advantage economically from his higher stock of cultural capital. Indeed, Bloom seems better off economically and so he can with some justification set against Stephen's university education the notion of having an equally good training at the "university of life" (*U*, 682, l.34; 17.555). The book thus contributes to that wonderful mystification promoted often this century to deny that college allows some in society an unfair advantage: the notion that university education is training in obscure subjects and so makes people unfit to get ahead economically. The novel ignores completely and even covers up the economic advantage conferred by a university education, obscuring the fact that this novel is structured in its center around the central marker of class difference in the twentieth century, the contrast between high school and university education. By converting a central marker of class difference into a "cultural difference" the novel serves to deny there is any need to educate the poor or any need to expand university admission. This is a crucial postcolonial issue—how much should the postcolonial regime make an effort to educate those who have not been allowed into the colonial educational system?

Once we notice how thoroughly Joyce's novel is structured around the meeting of opposed "classes," we can see that Rushdie's novel is in large scale structured similarly. The books opens in the world of the wealthy and ends in the world of the poor and presents both as full of good people with simply "different" kinds of knowledge. It starts with a doctor gaining access to family wealth via his expertise, his university education, and ends in the Magicians' Ghetto, described as slum but full of people with remarkable abilities that could never be learned in a university. Both groups function to provide the prime value of fiction: they are "interesting." The fact that one kind of education leads to great wealth and the other does not fades away as we are "educated" as readers to agree with Saleem, there is good and bad in all forms of education.

These books might even be considered to provide experiences of class tourism, as they have clearly functioned to provide experiences of ethnic tourism. Class tourism is not as strange as it sounds: movies often exploit the humor of the truck driver forced to sit through an opera, or the art critic appalled at a demolition derby. In *Ulysses* and *Midnight's Children,* excursions into other classes abound: Bloom enjoys thinking about operas; Stephen finds it amusing to speak over the heads of lower-class sailors in an alley; Saleem travels to the homes of the rich and powerful and to the hovels of the always picturesque poor (as the name Picture Singh reminds us). These novels present finely articulated examples of class tourism, for their readers as for their characters.

They are of course more than simply travel books: they take us into worlds we do not know and convince us of the value of those worlds, and so seem to contribute to social justice and reduction of prejudice. The sadness at the ends of these novels are in large part sadness at the unfair treatment of the lower classes. In creating sympathy for the poor, anger at their mistreatement, and a sense of how interesting they are, these novels then seem to support the progressive movement toward elimination of class inequities; a number of critics have argued such a line—for example, I did in my book *Modernism and Mass Politics: Joyce, Woolf, Eliot, Yeats* (Tratner 1995). I still believe these novels accomplish some of that purpose; but at the same time, they obscure the fact that prejudice is not simply blindness, but rather a system of misunderstanding that is at least connected to, if not created by, structures of wealth and power which do not change as a direct result of changes in attitude. The goal of understanding across class and ethnic barriers that permeates these novels is a valuable intellectual goal; the relationship of the way these novels pursue that goal to politics remains a deep and vexing question. For one thing, it seems that in these novels hybridity largely functions as a way to produce aesthetic pleasure, not political action or material change, and so these novels may contribute to the transformation of demands for power and material equality into demands for cultural expression, foreshadowing the strange contradiction of the world today, in which postcolonial literature has become a huge world market at the same time that postcolonial nations sink under the effects of neoclassical world economics: postmodern cultural liberation—hybridity—may then substitute for and help resist economic and political liberation.

7

Postcolonial Cartographies

The Nature of Place in Joyce's *Finnegans Wake* and in Friel's *Translations*

CHRISTY L. BURNS

IN HIS ESSAY "IRELAND AND THE ARTS" (1901), W. B. Yeats observed that Ireland was rich in legends and natural beauty, and he urged writers and artists to "master this history, these legends, and fix upon their memory the appearance of mountains and rivers and make it all visible again in their arts, so that Irishmen, even though they had gone thousands of miles away, would still be in their own country" (Yeats 1997, 336). In the 1930s, Daniel Corkery argued that a national literature for Ireland must engage on three levels: it must address the religious consciousness of the people, it must inspire nationalist sentiments, and it must relate itself to the land (Corkery 1931, 19). James Joyce's writing addresses the first two of Corkery's requisites, although he is often dissident in his treatment of conventional Irish values. Yet while Joyce is insistent on placing his work in Ireland long after he takes up residence on the Continent, his focus is most often on the city (Dublin) or on interpersonal and communal tensions. The appreciation of natural beauty hardly suits Joyce's critical agenda. So when Stephen Dedalus describes the artist's discernment, in his description of Aquinas's definition of beauty in *A Portrait of the Artist as Young Man,* his example of natural reality is a basket of apples, not an Irish hillside or glen. One could ask where we might place writers who, like Joyce, are far removed from the homeland as they write, and are urbanites into the bargain. For Joyce is now accepted as part of the Irish literary canon and a figure in postcolonial studies. Yet the issue of the land remains one that divides him not only from Yeats, but from contemporary Irish writers such as Brian Friel and Seamus Heaney. I suggest here that Joyce's postmodern treatment of language combines with his approach to cartography, in *Finnegans Wake,* in a manner that redefines Irish postcolonialism, moving it away from nationalist-homeland concerns and toward a diasporic position.

In my discussion of Joyce's particular brand of postcolonialism, I focus on "locale" as an important crux in his final work, where something like Yeats's imaginative engagement with the land and myth is replaced with a radically complex set of relations that challenges a more immediate correspondence between land and imagination. In his treatment of cartography, Joyce remaps space through linguistic reshapings, across bodies, and as simultaneous reference to two or more distant spaces, such as Dublin and America. After Fredric Jameson's call in the 1980s for a new cartography of postmodern spaces, intellectual mapping has become an urgent project (Jameson 1984); Joyce's work on it in the 1920s and 1930s was prescient in its radical nature. In contrast to the colonizing nature of England's attempts to map Ireland, Joyce's cartography in *Finnegans Wake* evades the will to control and multiplies identities and verbal references in a way that embraces a postmodern refusal of essences. Indeed, if mimetic representation can further colonial control of a country, then the postmodern defines a kind of postcolonial consciousness that moves beyond the internalized polarities that are the legacy of colonization. The conflict that these two cartographies (postmodern and imperialist) reveal might be between postcolonialism and a narrow form of nationalism.

To better define these terms in *Finnegans Wake,* which has an admittedly broad and mobile form of mapping both geographic and historical elements, I set Joyce's last work off against a reading of Brian Friel's play, *Translations* (1981), which rewrites the history of England's attempts to map and rename the Irish in the mid–nineteenth century. Anthony Roche has identified Friel as, after Beckett, "the most important Irish playwright" since the Abbey Theatre's celebrated beginnings, citing both his dramatic achievements and cultural significance for Ireland (2006, 1). An Irish playwright from the North, Friel wrote the *Translations* as he was moving into "the militancy of Field Day," a theatre troupe he co-founded with Stephen

Rea (Pine 1999, 22). Friel's work is postmodern in many ways, and two years later he retracted the play's narrower form of nationalism by writing and staging *The Communication Cord,* which parodies and mocks sentimentality about things "authentically" Irish. Nonetheless, even in *Translations,* one experiences Friel's effort to balance between postcolonial and nationalist possibilities. After using this play to define some of the tensions within the Irish literary emphasis on locale, I turn to *Finnegans Wake* to suggest that Joyce's own postmodern form of cartography connects the emphasis on place to that of language. Joyce's project differs from Friel's own treatment of language in his notoriously radical de-essentialization of meaning. Instead of reclaiming place names and identifying the land as the essential founding place of Irish identity, Joyce reconstitutes Irish culture as something that, while imaginatively tethered to Ireland, maintains more in the materiality of the word; the word is likened to Ireland in that its brute materiality resists being fully mastered—by the British who endeavor to use it for their own ends. It resists intention, turning back to its sensate components: the visual, aural (regional accent), and tactile aspects of language.

❧

Early in Homi Bhabha's work on stereotyping in colonial discourses, he observed that colonialists attempt to fix or ossify the image of the other so as to suppress their own inner sense of psychological and social disorder (Bhabha 1983a, 18). Just as racist stereotypes bear the brunt of the drive by colonialists to purify themselves, maps of contested territories necessarily reveal the imprint of such a struggle. In studies of cartography, maps have long been understood as more than scientific sketches of geography; they are instead reflections of the will to revise an empire's interpretation of reality. Christopher Board, in "Maps as Models," describes maps as analytical tools that enable their makers to see the real world in a new light—or to completely re-envision reality (Board 1967, 672). Graham Huggan extends this point to suggest that a map can function as a tool of persuasion, demonstrating, at its most extreme, the fantasy that the world can be turned into a simple object (Huggan 1994, 5). Medieval and ancient maps often recorded belief more obviously than fact, so that the "new 'scientific' cartography" of the seventeenth and eighteenth centuries, though informed by more precise means of measurement and of attaining accuracy, still operated primarily as a tool of the colonialist imagination—and this practice continued into the nineteenth century (Huggan 1994, 8). These "mimetic" documents present an artificially stabilized perspective of terrain that was in fact culturally fragmented, with marginalized groups erased or renamed, and any alternative view that might threaten those in power invariably suppressed.

Early cartographical projects failed, however, to control or clarify Ireland. David J. Baker describes the Renaissance project of mapping Ireland as a nearly comic attempt on England's part to stabilize what refused to be mimetically static and clear. "English mapping," he argues "was not a one-sided affair, but a complex attempt to create coherence in a space populated by antagonistic and elusive 'others' who . . . left their traces, their erasures on every chart" (Baker 1993, 79). The English habit of hiring "hostile monoglot Gaelic speakers to identify the half-forgotten meanings of a depopulated and overgrown countryside" left a cartographical project that revealed implicitly its own contested nature. Baker observes that the final product was merely a rough amalgamate that showed the fragmentation and various modes of resistance that marred the Queen's attempt to control the space through representational force (78, 81–82). The early nineteenth-century maps sponsored by England were therefore not the first attempts to nail down the Irish terrain and claim cultural, linguistic, and geographic dominance of the land. And it is no coincidence that the main crisis for contemporary Ireland is partition—the remapping of the territory into British-allied and Republic portions of the Island.

Karl Marx commented that "The Irish question is . . . not simply a nationality question, but a question of land and existence" (Marx and Engels 1972, 142). With the history of invasion and later problems of evictions of poor, predominantly Catholic farming tenants off of Anglo-Irish land, the physicality of the land itself is as crucial as its images and associations. The history of British mapping of Ireland is therefore wrought with antagonisms. The land is linked to language use, on account of the renaming of places that occurred in a series of surveys and cartographical projects launched by the English. Thomas Davis, of the Young Ireland Movement, argued that the imposition of the English language was a kind of "deterritorialisation" that usurped the identity of Irish places (Lloyd 1993, 158). Seamus Heaney, more recently, has suggested that one gets a "sense of place" from a writer's work if it evokes not only the beauty of the land, but its particular oral history. Thus, a place name can call up not only the geographical country, but the "country of the mind" that "takes its tone unconsciously from a shared oral inherited culture, or from a consciously savoured literary culture, or from both" (Heaney 1980, 132).

Brian Friel's critique of the British "translation" of Ireland into an anglicized map, in *Translations,* demonstrates the troubled and urgent link between language and the land. The play addresses the Ordnance Survey of Ireland from 1824 to 1846 and explicitly draws on John Andrews's study, *The Paper Landscape: The Ordnance Survey in Nineteenth-Century Ireland* (1975). Set in 1833 in Baile Beag, a fictional Donegal border town in Northern Ireland, the story opens with the commencement of lessons in a hedge school, where only Latin, Greek, and Gaelic are spoken; it closes with the collapse of the community, which has been militarily disrupted by British soldiers and culturally dispersed as the hedge school fails to compete with the "new national school," where books are free and only English will be spoken (Friel 1981, 23). *Translations* is therefore not only about mapping but also about colonial violence and the erasure of local languages. It is, moreover, crucially about the nature of history writing, even as it is also a controversial fictionalization of Irish history.[1]

In Friel's play, British soldiers wind up destroying an Irish community, but Ireland's offenders are not immediately easy to sort by nationality. The young British Lieutenant, George Yolland, falls instantly in love with the Irish landscape, but his Irish coworker, Owen O'Donnell, is more cynical about the area's charms and his role in helping the British rename it.

1. The play itself has been harshly criticized by some for its rewriting of Irish history. Kurt Bullock accuses Friel of "myopia" and of violating a kind of integrity, as he reshapes history (Bullock 2000, 110, 103–6). While a British surveyor did meet with Yolland's fate, he points out that this was in 1602, not 1833, and no destruction of land and eviction of Irish occurred during the surveys, according to Bullock (102). Friel has, however, argued for the force of this revisionary history, which is compelled more toward the present and future of Ireland, and so must imaginatively reshape its past in this dramatic production. Michael Mays points out that Friel "subtly but insistently draws attention to the centrality of memory in those processes by which histories—official and otherwise—are cobbled together out of the heterogeneous fragments of the nation's prehistory" (2005, 2).

"My job," as Owen explains, "is to translate the quaint archaic tongue you people persist in speaking to the King's good English" (Friel 1981, 32). He is a self-described "part-time, underpaid civilian interpreter" who grew up in Baile Beag. Setting up Yolland as the spokesperson for Baile Beag's charms—and those of the Irish language and place names as well—Friel casts that position of ardor for the beauty of Ireland as one of naïveté and even, potentially, misapprehension.

A tensional link springs up between the imagination of Ireland and its immediate, physical ground—between the land and its image. This reaches beyond the problem of the 1833 mapping of Ireland to a more general problem embedded in the English imagination of the island. Declan Kiberd claims that "if Ireland had never existed, the English would have invented it; and since it never existed in English eyes as anything more than a patchwork-quilt of warring fiefdoms, their leaders occupied the neighbouring island and called it Ireland. With the mission to impose a central administration went the attempt to define a unitary Irish character. . . . Ireland was soon patented as not-England, a place whose peoples were, in many important ways, the very antithesis of their new rulers from overseas" (Kiberd 1996, 9). Irish identity is not some originary essence that colonization had destroyed. Prior to Strongbow's assault and the series of Protestant "plantings" in Ireland, the country was already *post*modern in its fragmentary culture and political divisions. This does not remove the necessity now of a postcolonial struggle to come to terms with a fractured identity and a history of oppression and disenfranchisement. What it does suggest is that the reach back to Irish "origins" becomes postmodern as a writer looks more toward the past; those more strongly tethered to the *contemporary* political moment may wind up being more modern, in their mourning of a lost sense of wholeness, imaginary as that moment of originary unity may well be.[2] Sentimentalizing the land can be a way of finding a foundational wholeness, a desire that writers like Joyce treat as suspect.

2. In their commentary on the continuing influence of W. B. Yeats's vision of a "Unity of Culture," Mark and James Farrelly turn to Friel's later plays as one place where the tensions in culture and consciousness, made explicit in Yeats's writing, re-emerge. See Farrelly and Farrelly 1998, 105–6.

Friel responds to the opposition of imagination and land by turning to language. The anglicization of Gaelic place names was one crucial aspect of British cartography on the island. Friel finds a second, kindred tension: the sound and evocative link to memories in a word (its familiarity) mark it differently than its function as a referent. Its content matters, of course, but so does its "body" or embodiment in language. The body of the word—and its evocative effect—can be in tension with its signifying function, so that translation that is merely literal loses this important aspect. In *Translations,* Owen and Yolland are charged with anglicizing the Gaelic names of landmarks in the area, either by translating the roots of names into English or by following the sound, in Gaelic, to some approximate English sound. So Bun na hAbhann, which names a small point where a stream enters the sea, can be translated into Bunowen, which Owen confesses is "somehow neither fish nor flesh." It can alternately be named "Burnfoot." Yolland resists this renaming, wanting to find an equivalent to the sound of the word as well. Eventually, he likens their work to "an eviction of sorts" and complains that "something is being eroded" (Friel 1981, 51). Holding onto a name's transliteral referent while losing its Gaelic embodiment disturbs the British lieutenant, but here changing even the sound of Gaelic into the English sound is a loss as well. Hugh—the hedge school's master and also Owen's father—tells Yolland that Gaelic "is a rich language, Lieutenant, full of the mythologies of fantasy and hope and self-deception—a syntax opulent with tomorrows. It is our response to mud cabins and a diet of potatoes; our only method of replying to . . . inevitabilities" (50). By the close of the second act, a powerful nostalgia for Gaelic language haunts the stage, and it upstages, in that sense, the sentimental emphasis on the land.

Friel does not rest his nationalist play upon a single hybrid construct—that of the Ireland replaced and reinscribed through anglicization. He adds to this problem another emotion—that of love. In *Finnegans Wake,* desire often brings about a "translation" of the self; at one point a voice calls on a lover to "transname me loveliness, now and here me for all times!" (*FW,* 145.21), requesting both translation (or change) and location—"now and here me." In *Translations,* Yolland falls in love with more than the surrounding land and culture of Baile Beag; he falls in love with Maire Chatach, loving the sight of her and the sound of her voice, without any transliteral understanding of her

Irish speech. Their love scene, at the close of Act II, turns upon the part of language that is left off when words and names are only literally translated. She understands no English, and he no Gaelic. Through sound alone, by naming local places, they finally converse:

> YOLLAND: . . . Druim Dubn?(MAIRE *stops. She is listening.* YOLLAND *is encouraged.*) Poll na gCaorach. Lis Maol. (MAIRE *turns toward him.*) Lis na nGall.
>
> MAIRE: Lis na nGradh. *(They are now facing each other and begin moving—almost imperceptibly—towards one another.)* Carraig an Phoill.
>
> YOLLAND: Carraig na Ri. Loch na nEan.
>
> MAIRE: Loch an Iubhair. Machaire Buidhe.
>
> YOLLAND: Machaire Mor. Cnoc na Mona.
>
> MAIRE: Cnoc na nGabhar.
>
> YOLLAND: Mullach.
>
> MAIRE: Port.
>
> YOLLAND: Tor.
>
> MAIRE: Lag. (61–62)

The embodiment of sound (rather than meaning) in words enables the lovers to connect and "communicate" in the simplest referential manner, one that points only toward the land; Yolland and Maire, if they cannot exchange conceptual meanings, want at least to hear voice and words. They understand each purely in cartographical terms; later on we will discover that Yolland has traced a map in the sand and has shown Maire where Winfarthing, his hometown in England, is (72). To her, he is knowable because she can locate his home on a map, just as earlier in the play she endeavored to know America by sketching its shape (21). Geography thus takes on a naïvely essentialist role in establishing familiarity and a sense of identity (in origins and space). Seamus Deane argues that "only in the Yolland-Maire moment does language truly speak; it is only then that language is beyond translations" (Deane 1993, 109). Dean has conceptualized language's role as "to nominate, to specify the context in which human love is possible. It is at that level that 'culture' and 'politics', Irish are English, are reconciled. Everything else is 'after'—the world of division is, in a sense, always anachronistic" (109). While the play delivers sentiment in support of this assertion, it also undercuts any faith in this imaginative leap "beyond" the navigation of differences. Ultimately,

Maire and Yolland have exchanged the sensuous shell of language that, though hardly trivial, leaves aside the kind of "knowing" that meanings can convey—as well as evocation of oral history, such as Heaney desires. There is no translation in this relationship, only a rapturous "knowing" that evades any hermeneutic negotiation of difference and of the misapprehensions upon which language insists. Imagination may momentarily appear potent and "beyond" difference in Yolland and Maire's exchange, but the evocation of language and accents are not those of true memory here. They are simply an appreciation for the aesthetic and sensate experience of the moment, devoid of any attachment to deeper mutual knowledge, historical or psychological. The land is familiar to Maire, but new and exotic to Yolland. Act III of *Translations* returns to the failure of such imagination, and the immediate urgency of violence and conflict over control of the land itself.

Maire's knowledge of Yolland, thin and wistful as it may be, is abruptly terminated by his disappearance and supposed murder, the night after he walks her home from a dance. When Yolland's superior officer is unable to locate him, he warns the villagers that the British will destroy the corn and livestock in revenge for this death, just as in reality they would forcibly patrol the land and enforce British law. A return to the essentialization of land threatens, but does not wholly arrive. Likewise, a fierce patrolling of racial boundaries commences, as Jimmy (a learned older Irishman) warns Maire that she must marry within the "tribe" or race: "Do you know the Greek word *endogamein*?" Jimmy asks Maire. "It means to marry within the tribe. And the word *exogamein* means to marry outside the tribe. And you don't cross those borders casually" (Friel 1981, 82). To avoid violence, one must comprehend the difference within language, rather than appreciate its mere outer aspect. One must also adhere to tradition, even when it involves prejudicial negations of foreigners and difference. Hugh, the schoolmaster, ends the play dramatically, twice reciting lines about Juno's love of an ancient city, Lybia, which was to be other-thrown by the Trojans (83). In this closing moment, Friel creates an ultranationalist play, charging England with erasing a glorious city and nation. However, the ending is shadowed by the play's earlier, complex construction of the relations between essence and imagination, between cultures and their translations from past into present.

Jimmy's love of Greek literature and mythology takes a suspect turn toward personal interpolation. Observing the magnificence of Athene as she transforms Ulysses into an old man, Jimmy finds in the text a mirror of his own aging physical appearance. Even as Manus, Hugh's other son, reminds Jimmy that Athene was a goddess, not human and among them, Jimmy likens her as well to a local woman, thus believing imaginary constructs from literature and myth to be real in his present life. Prejudice and entrapment converge here, as Jimmy draws too stark a link between concepts and their literal embodiments. Hugh consequently remarks to Owen, "James thinks he knows [where he lives]. I look at James and three thoughts occur to me: A—that it is not the literal past, the 'facts' of history, that shape us, but images of the past embodied in language. James has ceased to make that discrimination" (80). And then "B—we must never cease renewing those images; because once we do, we fossilize" (81). Here, Friel negotiates between the powerful nostalgia for "home" and origins—which might be more closely identified with modernism—and a postmodern discrimination between "true" history and its necessary refunctioning on behalf of cultural imaginations. Jimmy has lost the distinction between fact and imagination, believing that the Greek gods are present in his reality, that literature can be fully interpolated into his life and existence. Friel walks a careful line between such erasures of distinction and radical opposition. His seemingly modern art, which holds closer to nostalgia for a prior wholeness, glances briefly toward postmodern history and Joyce's more radical "renewing" in *Finnegans Wake.*

Modern and postmodern writing differs, in matter of degree, as to how it approaches the function of words. Here, language can be understood as being directed toward: (1) its imaginative, culturally relevant effects (invoking memory, Irish myth, the Famine), (2) mere sensate shell, or (3) self-conscious, intended meaning (nationalist message). And the unconscious implications (metaphor, parapraxis) may also reveal unintended significance. Modernism emerges after Freud has begun to cast light on the limitations of self-conscious intention. If modernists are sometimes described as engaged in willful self-making (after Ezra Pound's famous edict, "Make It New"), much of modern literature embraces the other three aspects of language, drawing close to postmodernism's fuller embrace of disruptive elements. A postmodernist will be wary of any attempt to nail down a one-to-one correspondence between content and material form, seeing this gesture as akin to colonial mapping, which distorts and sorts things into black and white, friend and foe. Although *Finnegans Wake* (1939) was published during the modernist period, it exhibits more postmodern tendencies than Friel's play; it also distances from ultranationalist gestures while offering up a more realistic image of identity as multiple and split, a form of identity potentially appropriate to postcolonial consciousness.

In his discussion of the postmodern condition, Jean-François Lyotard defends experimentalism and its critique of consensus and norms. Casting aside the usual periodization (modern to postmodern), he argues that "a work can become modern only if it is first postmodern," and postmodernism becomes not modernism's end but its nascent state (Lyotard 1992, 13). A modern work must challenge the assumption of the presentable, and so open up the space for the unpresentable to emerge. Lyotard distinguishes the sliver of difference between the two practices as that between regret and experimentation. Citing Joyce and Proust, he observes that they invoke and pursue the unpresentable, in consciousness or, for Joyce, in language itself. Postmodernists will eschew standard realism, as a repressive form of consensus, and they will interrogate the drive toward metanarratives (and the claims founded upon them). And more dispositionally, as Anthony Appiah's analysis reveals, postmodernism repeatedly rejects the exclusivism of such movements as Enlightenment thought, with its emphasis on rationality, essentialism, elitism, and authoritarianism (Appiah 1992). In this manner, the postmodernist is akin to the postcolonialist, in so far as she is able to exorcise the shadow of the tyrant initially internalized through resistance. If the colonized has learned opposition and blanket rejection from the colonizer, the postmodern postcolonialist mocks the oppositional urge as yet another recycling of authoritarian exclusivism. How then to map from the postcolonial perspective, from the position of a country, like Ireland, which has been so often subjected to the colonizing force of cartography?

❧

The project of mapping Ireland, with all its essentializing insistence on the foundational importance of the land, runs into its greatest obscurity in the *Wake*. The book's opening pages sketch a map (via the riverrun) not only of Dublin and Howth's head, reaching out toward Armorica; they also map these regions over a resettled Irish community in Lauren's County, Georgia, in the United States. The *Wake* is more than haunted by a diaspora's imagination of a lost country; Joyce's own project of recalling nursery rhymes, barroom songs, and stories his father told resonates with the exile's nostalgic imagination. Rather than construct a false, singular image, Joyce allows that a mobile bricolage, peopled by associative character-ghosts who repeatedly shift shape, might be the dream that the slumbering Irishman has of home. So even as the *Wake* maps Ireland through the diasporic imagination, such references always point in a variety of directions. The book's title is taken in part from that of an Irish-American ballad (*Finnegan's Wake*). It is also, famously, punning on the invocation of war (Finnegans Wake!) as well as the wake of that American hod-layer, Finnegan. It is both at home and abroad, at once. Moreover, it plays in the nightworld, its imagination evading the solidified symbols of conscious art. Language drifts through parapraxes and verbal slippages, so that the interpretation of "nation" and home become equally changeable.

In *Joyce's Book of the Dark*, John Bishop provides various Wakean maps: of Dublin, of linguistic associations, of Europe, and most significantly a map of "Howth Castle and Environs," that is "Dublin by Daylight," which Bishop pairs with a "Relief Map B" of the novel's nightworld. Both maps are sketched with the language of the *Wake,* so that each bears scant resemblance to "real" current-day maps of the city. Bishop notes, with his wry humor, that as the book opens we are given merely "a representational smokescreen that sustains the misleading appearance of vague consonance with waking reality," whereas in fact we are witnessing dream, as "latent content" of what derives from "matters that fall under the ban of our infrarational senses" (*FW,* 19.36–20.1; Bishop 1986, 36). Just as sleep marks a numbing of the senses and a loss of the "real" world, so dreams constitute a new world, drawn out of the sleeper's body (Bishop 1986, 37). Bishop ventures: "A writer of strong realist allegiances, as the evidence of everything he wrote before *Finnegans Wake* attests, Joyce would have beheld in the darker parts of sleep the paradoxical spectacle of an undeniably real human experience ("you were there") within which 'reality,' 'experience,' and all human knowing mutually vanished into a state that the *Wake* calls, with contradictory precision, 'Real Absence' (*FW,* 536.5–6)" (43).

If memory is present as a "Real Absence" in the *Wake,* the experiences of postcolonial and diasporic desires are pervasive. Joyce's form of imagination becomes radically distinct from those of the Romantics and of Yeats's early symbolic and mythic treatment of Ireland. Symbolic categories do not maintain, and any identifications are pulled associatively sideways. This is Descartes's nightmare: in sleep the peripheries that define us dissolve. And so, in essence, the boundaries the mark out Irish terrain are also absent (even if the wars are not).

In "When Buckley Shot the Russian General" (*FW,* II, iii), the dangers of conflating memory with imagination emerge as a misunderstanding transforms a moment of mixed sympathy into violence as the result of one small, accidental gesture. Butt and Taff, in their radio play, have just arrived at the moment of climax. Butt "apoxyomenously deturbaned" relays the story of how an Irish soldier, who has a general in his rifle sites, hesitates to kill the man as he is squatting in mid-defecation. Just as the Irishman's pity is about to win out, the general reaches for a bit of sod and uses it to wipe himself. The Irishman, identifying the clump as Irish land, is immediately enraged: "Yastsar! In sabre tooth and sobre saviles! Senonnevero! That he leaves nyet is my grafe. He deared me to it and he dared me do it, and bedattle I didaredonit . . . beheaving up that sob of tunf for to claimhis, for to wollpimsolff, puddywhuck. Ay, and untuoning his culothone in an exitous erseroyal *Deo Jupto.* At that instullt to Igorladns! Prronto! I gave one dobblenotch and I ups with my crozzier. Mirrdo! With my how on armer and hits leg an arrow cockshock rockrogn. Sparro!" (*FW,* 353.9–21). The general's commandeering of a (very small) piece of the land—which he wipes shit with—delivers an unintended insult to "Igorlands." Unfortunately for the general, his gesture resonates with a repeated narrative of disdainful appropriation that the Irish nationalist remembers and from which his imagination abstracts. Note that the language fuses, as the Irishman becomes more enraged. The words become more immediately referential, imitating the sound of a shot (cockshock rockrogn. Sparro!), even as their conceptual references are multidirectional and obscured. The gunshot could fire off in any direction, but the sound of violence will accompany every trajectory. In distinction to Friel's treatment of language in the Yolland-Maire exchange, Joyce's sensate words create another level of reference—that of action. Words may be purely pleasurable at times, but Joyce's emphasis on their materiality frequently doubles back as violence. His words thus function as multiply referential and immediate (sensory) mimesis (loud sounds and violence). In this way, Joyce opens the range of language's potential signifying functions and allows the word to become plastic, something other than the transparent medium through which one reads. "Buckley" is just one sod-centered episode among many, in the *Wake,* in which Joyce mocks the Irish nationalist's essentialism and the violence toward which it tends.

At the opening of an earlier chapter (in the children's "Night Lessons"—260–266 of II, ii), the sons, who are often at war with one another, are mutually lost. They consult a map of Dublin—possibly learning geography—and work their way back to their father's inn, in Chapelizod (Glasheen 1977, xlix). The tale opens with a "we" who wonder where they are "from tomtittot to teetootomtotalitarian" (*FW,* 260.2), which takes them from tot to totalitarian, or from youth to patriarchal rule. This could be a message to the father (the patriarch), or the story of maturation, a biographical history from babe's youth to a full, wise backward glance at history. They muse that "Whom will comes over" (*FW,* 260.4), suggesting that whomever wishes might come to invade (or for a visit). One strand of narrative stutter here is the history of Ireland and invasions. The sons' thoughts replay the opening and closing of the *Wake* itself, from "Long Livius Lane, mid Mezzofanti Mall" through various byways, ending up at "New Livius Lane till where we whiled while we whithered" (*FW,* 260.9–10, 13–14). They move through both history (Livius was a historian; McHugh 1991, 260) and geography, recognizing the linguist's (Mezzofanti) influence. Joyce often double-maps time and space, yet his manner of attaching history to the land is not as clean and direct as in Heaney's formulation of a "sense of place." Joyce's is, rather, an awareness of the simultaneous negotiation. The sons decide to "let bygones be bei Gunne's" with the father, upon whom they contemplate war (*FW,* 263.17–18), and they declare the need for "olderwise" "since primal made alter in garden of Idem," punning on 'Eden' and sameness (Latin; *FW,* 263.19–20). Wise old men (be they God, the "Groupname for grape-juice" *FW,* 261.f3, or the father, HCE) are necessary. This passage briefly celebrates the land, stream and mountain (*FW,* 261.3)—rivers and salmon (*FW,* 264.6–7, 17)—but without making it essential. Dublin also is declared a "phantom city" that has been "bowed and sould" "for a price partitional of twenty six and six" (*FW*, 264.19, 20, 22–23). Joyce thus intersperses praise of Ireland's beauty with hints of the wars that mark it, and the partition, in 1922, that remapped it, dividing the country in two. The twins, Shem and Shaun, likewise contemplate their various (dis)identities, echoing the tension between likeness and difference, which Joyce replays in scenarios of aggression between the sons (as well as against the father) throughout the *Wake*. While repeatedly reinscribing this history of aggression, Joyce refuses to embrace a foundational understanding of the land. His conception of interpersonal dynamics may be framed by the oppositional consciousness inherited from colonialism, but he loosens the inevitability of that duality in his parodic critique of its inherit violence. As he pulls away from a more modernist form of (post)colonial consciousness, Joyce multiplies possible identities in a way that destabilizes reifications, thereby moving his last text into a more postmodern understanding of postcoloniality.

In Shaun's Third Watch (*FW*, III, iii), mapping is less a helpful enterprise and more a reductive attempt, on the part of the Four (corners of Ireland, and the judges as well), who are endeavoring to force sleepy Yawn to awake and transform into the father. Yawn lies gargantuan, "On the mead of the hillock lay, heartsoul dormant mid shadowed landshape" (*FW*, 474.1–3). He is sleepily stretched over Ireland but also, in another cast, on the (and AS the) hill of Uisnech, where the four counties of Ireland meet. The four (mamalujo, the four gospels, the four judges, or the counties) converge upon him: "Themselves came at him, from the westborders of the eastmidlands, three kings of three suits and a crowner" (*FW*, 474.17–19). Yawn lies "one half of him in Conn's half but the whole of him nevertheless in Owenmore's five quarters"(*FW*, 475.6–7). The Four seek their identity in him, as they "clomb together" over him to interrogate him. This is not just Ireland examining itself, but also England mapping: "For he was ever their quarrel, the way they would see themselves" (*FW*, 475.19–20). It is night, however, and the Four's senses are "ensorcelled" so that they cannot "tell their heels from their stools" as they crouch down to question Yawn (*FW*, 476.29, 30). As "question time drew nighing and the map of the souls groupography rose in relief within their quarterings," they endeavor to crystallize their (Irish) identity (*FW*, 476.33–5). As I explain in *Gestural Politics*, Yawn refuses their attempts to make him call forth the father and to consolidate his sleepy identity. Here, Joyce plays out the necessity of a elision of reified identity—whether called up by the Irish (Sinn Féin) or the British (mapping). Yawn's is a wily Irishness, refusing to be mapped and analyzed as Other. And he turns repeatedly to the senses, calling for his "pipette" or dear one, as well as the "Typette, my tactile O!" (*FW,* 478.27). Language comically distracts him from the nationalist call for reification, so that he lolls in love with the flirtatious word, and the hermeneutic agenda of the Four is blocked in consequence of this attachment to materiality. This is not, as in Friel, a materiality that unites; instead, it is sensory language that distracts from meaning as based on oppositional construct.

Joyce's map of Ireland is thus a "langscape" (*FW,* 595.04), a map that is shaped more by words (and their material resistances) than by geographic boundaries. As such, it points both toward the project of reclaiming Irish identity through the study and teaching of Gaelic, implicitly. More emphatically, however, and in critique of that project's drive to recollect purity, it pursues a postmodern approach to postcoloniality, which understands perception and culture to be shaped by language. Jacques Lacan's famous edict that "the unconscious is structured like a language" is not exclusively Lacan's own insight; it expresses an emerging understanding that grew out of anthropological research that informed social and linguistic understandings as Modernism was beginning to wane. In the late 1950s, Lacan insisted that there were no possibilities of exchange "even if unconscious" outside "the permutations authorized by language" (Lacan 1977b, 20; 1977a, 148). Language signifies more than a referent; it can, in Joyce's work, collect scattered possibilities and contain contradictions, much as culture—as the unconscious coalescence of memories and various forms of meaning—began to function more as a broad net that now tentatively connects disparate groups together. Thus, one can understand Ireland itself now as a location for many displaced foreign workers, as well as comprehend Irishness as an extended cultural consciousness that reaches across national boundaries as its thin threads follow its own diaspora abroad.

In *Finnegans Wake,* this odd collection is Irish, European, Egyptian . . . and diasporic. The *Wake*'s final recourso opens (*FW,* 593.2) with a rallying call "calling all downs," which invokes not only "all daynes to dawn" (*FW,*

593.11), but also the resurrection of all fallen figures. It more consistently hails the coming of the day (days to dawn) and the recirculation of time. Geographically, the sun rises on Earwicker and Ireland, as well as the whole world, signaling Joyce's method of simultaneous micro- and macro-mapping: "Eireweeker to the wohld bludyn world" (*FW*, 593.3). Anger-land is Ireland or a weeklong commencement of ire. It is also the father figure, HCE or Earwicker, who has become weaker through the night. What is individuated is also always culturally expansive in the *Wake*. As McHugh observes, "bludyn" is an anagram for dublyn, making the whole bloody world also the whole dublyn world. Moreover, the word itself becomes active in this awakening of Earwicker, Ireland, and world. The passage calls for the guardian's return (Arcthuris) and also Arthur's, foretelling that he will be a "verb umprincipiant through the trancitive spaces" (*FW*, 594.2–3). Such unprincipled (and unprecipitated) language will be transitive, engaging spaces in movement rather than cartographical stasis. Soon it is also suggested that this guardian or king will wake to a scene that is either Irish or Persian or placed in New Ireland: "Whake? Hill of Hafid, knock and knock, nachasac . . ." (*FW*, 595.3). The Hill of Howth and its hills ("knock" meaning a hill) are here, but references to Hafid (a king of Persia) and to New Ireland follow on the heels of these hills. However one determines this map or space, the passage asserts that being there "gives relief to the langscape" as he stretches toward New Ireland. A map that stretches toward the New World may alleviate the fixity and aggression of colonial cartography, just as heterogeneous language undoes the labor of ultranationalist purification. As one voice hopefully proffers, "We may plesently heal Geoglyphy's twenty-nine ways of saying goodbett an wassing seoosoon liv" (*FW*, 595.6–8). We might presently (and pleasantly) hear or heal the twenty-nine ways in which "geoglyph"—the writing of the land (geography)—has of saying goodbye and singing "see you soon love" (or Livia). Irish literature thus waves farewell to its emigrants and hello again, when they return, say a "goodbett" in multiple tongues. The island renews, not only in terms of its historical memories linked to the countryside, but also in terms of the geographic links to the waves of Irish who leave and return.

Works Cited

Index

Works Cited

Adams, Robert Day. 1996. "Joyce's Aquacities." In *Joyce in the Hibernian Metropolis,* ed. Morris Beja and David Norris, 3–20. Columbus: Ohio State Univ. Press.

Amkpa, Awam. 1999. "Drama and the Languages of Postcolonial Desire: Bernard Shaw's Pygmalion." *Irish University Review: A Journal of Irish Studies* 29 (2): 294–304.

Andrews, J. H. 1975. *A Paper Landscape: The Ordnance Survey in Nineteenth-Century Ireland.* Oxford: Clarendon Press.

Anspaugh, Kelly. 1995. "Ulysses Upon Ajax? Joyce, Harrington, and the Question of 'Cloacal Imperialism'." *South Atlantic Review* 60 (2): 11–29.

Anzaldúa, Gloria. 1999. *Borderlands = La frontera.* San Francisco: Aunt Lute Books.

Appiah, Kwame Anthony. 1992. "The Postcolonial and the Postmodern." In *In My Father's House: Africa in the Philosophy of Culture,* 137–57. New York: Oxford Univ. Press.

Aravamudan, Srinivas. 1998. "Postcolonial Affiliations: *Ulysses* and All about H. Hatterr." In *Transcultural Joyce,* ed. Karen R. Lawrence, 97–128. Cambridge: Cambridge Univ. Press.

Armstrong, Paul B. 1996. "James Joyce and the Politics of Reading: Power, Belief, and Justice in 'Ulysses'." *B.A.S.: British and American Studies* 1 (1): 24–41.

Ashcroft, Bill, Gareth Griffiths, and Helen Tiffin. 1998. *Key Concepts in Post-Colonial Studies.* London: Routledge.

———. 1989. *The Empire Writes Back: Theory and Practice in Post-Colonial Literatures.* London: Methuen.

———, eds. 1995. *The Post-Colonial Studies Reader.* London: Routledge.

Attridge, Derek, and Marjorie Howes, eds. 2000. *Semicolonial Joyce.* Cambridge: Cambridge Univ. Press.

Avery, Bruce. 1995. "The Subject of Imperial Geography." In *Prosthetic Territories: Politics and Hypertechnologies,* ed. Gabriel Brahm Jr. and Mark Driscoll, 55–70. Boulder: Westview Press.

Bachorz, Stephanie. 2001. "Postcolonial Theory and Ireland: Revising Postcolonialism." In *Critical Ireland: New Essays in Literature and Culture,* ed. Alan A. Gillis and Aaron Kelly. Dublin: Four Courts.

Baker, David J. 1993. "Off the Map: Charting Uncertainty in Renaissance Ireland." In *Representing Ireland: Literature and the Origins of Conflict, 1534–1660,* ed. Brendan Bradshaw, Andrew Hadfield, Willy Maley, 76–92. New York: Cambridge Univ. Press.

Baucom, Ian. 1996. "Mournful Histories: Narratives of Postimperial Melancholy." *Modern Fiction Studies* 42 (2): 259–88.

Bhabha, Homi. 1983a. "The Other Question . . . : Homi Bhabha Reconsiders the Stereotype and Colonial Discourse." *Screen* 24:18–36.

———. 1983b. "Of Mimicry and Man: The Ambivalence of Colonial Discourse." In *Modern Literary Theory: A Reader,* ed. Philip Rice and Patricia Waugh, 360–68. New York: St. Martin's Press, 1996.

Bishop, John. 1986. *Joyce's Book of the Dark: Finnegans Wake.* Madison: Univ. of Wisconsin Press.

Board, Christopher. 1967. "Maps as Models." In Models in Geography, ed. R. Chorely and P. Haggett, 671–725. London: Methuen.

Boehmer, Elleke. 1995. *Colonial and Postcolonial Literature.* New York: Oxford Univ. Press.

Boland, Eavan. 1997. "Daughters of Colony: A Personal Interpretation of the Place of Gender Issues in the Postcolonial Interpretation of Irish Literature." *Æire-Ireland: A Journal of Irish Studies* 32 (2–3): 9–20.

Boltwood, Scott. 2002. "'An Emperor or Something': Brian Friel's *Columba,* Migrancy and Postcolonial Theory." *Irish Studies Review* 10 (1): 51–61.

Booker, M. Keith. 1996. "Decolonizing Literature: *Ulysses* and the Postcolonial Novel in English." In *Pedagogy, Praxis, Ulysses: Using Joyce's Text to Transform the Classroom,* ed. Robert Newman, 135–51. Ann Arbor: Univ. of Michigan Press.

———. 2000. *"Ulysses," Capitalism, and Colonialism: Reading Joyce after the Cold War.* Westport, Conn.: Greenwood Press.

Boon, James A. 1983. "Functionalists Write, Too: Frazer/Malinowski and the Semiotics of the Monograph." *Semiotica* 46:131–49.

Booth, Howard J., and Nigel Rigby, eds. 2000. *Modernism and Empire.* Manchester: Manchester Univ. Press.

Boyce, David G. 1995. *Nationalism in Ireland.* London: Routledge.

Bracher, Mark. 1993. *Lacan, Discourse and Social Change: A Psychoanalytic Cultural Criticism.* Ithaca: Cornell Univ. Press.

Budgen, Frank. 1972. *James Joyce and the Making of "Ulysses" and Other Writings.* Oxford: Oxford Univ. Press.

Bulfin, William. 1907. *Rambles in Eirinn.* 8th impression. Dublin: M. H. Gill and Son, 1929.

Bullock, Kurt. 2000. "Possessing Wor(l)ds: Brian Friel's *Translations* and the Ordinance Survey." *New Hibernian Review* 4 (2): 98–115.

Bulson, Eric. 2000. "An Italian Tongue in an Irish Mouth: Joyce, Politics, and the Franca Lingua." *Journal of Modern Literature* 24 (1): 63–79.

Burns, Christy L. 2000. *Gestural Politics: Stereotype and Parody in Joyce.* Albany: SUNY Press.

Bush, Ronald. 1998. "Rereading the Exodus: *Frankenstein, Ulysses, The Satanic Verses,* and Other Postcolonial Texts." In *Transcultural Joyce,* ed. Karen R. Lawrence, 129–47. Cambridge Univ. Press.

Buzard, James. 1993a. *The Beaten Track: European Tourism, Literature and the Ways to Culture.* Oxford: Oxford Univ. Press.

———. 1993b. "A Continent of Pictures: Reflections on the 'Europe' of Nineteenth-Century Tourists." *PMLA* 108:30–44.

———. 1996. "'Importunate Muchness': Intimations of Ethnography in James's European Tours." *Literature, Interpretation, Theory: LIT* 7:167–78.

———. 1999/2000. "'Culture' and the Critics of *Dubliners.*" *James Joyce Quarterly* 37 (1–2): 43–61.

Carroll, Clare, and Patricia King. 2003. *Ireland and Postcolonial Theory.* Notre Dame: Univ. of Notre Dame Press.

Castle, Gregory. 2001. *Modernism and The Celtic Revival.* Cambridge: Cambridge Univ. Press.

Cheng, Vincent J. 1992. "The General and the Sepoy: Imperialism and Power in the Museyroom." In *Critical Essays on James Joyce's* Finnegans Wake, ed. Patrick A. McCarthy, 258–68. New York: G. K. Hall.

———. 1995. *Joyce, Race, and Empire.* Cambridge: Cambridge Univ. Press.

———. 1997. "Of Canons, Colonies, and Critics: The Ethics and Politics of Postcolonial Joyce Studies." *Cultural Critique* 35 (Winter): 81–104.

———. 1998. "Of Canons, Colonies, and Critics: The Ethics and Politics of Postcolonial Joyce Studies." In *Re: Joyce: Text, Culture, Politics,* ed. John Brannigan, Geoff Ward, and Julian Walfreys. New York: Macmillan/St. Martin's, 224–45.

———. 2000. "Authenticity and Identity: Catching the Irish Spirit." In Attridge and Howes 2000, 240–61.

Chuang, Kun-liang. 1996. "Nation, Migrancy, and Identity: The Negotiation of a Third Space in Joyce's 'Ulysses,' Rushdie's 'The Satanic Verses' and Kingston's 'Tripmaster Monkey.'" *DAI* 57 (1): 200A.

Cleary, Joe. 2002. "Misplaced Ideas? Locating and Dislocating Ireland in Colonial and Postcolonial Studies." In *Marxism, Modernity, and Postcolonial Studies,* ed. Crystal Bartolovich and Neil Lazarus. Cambridge: Cambridge Univ. Press.

Clifford, James. 1997. *Routes: Travel and Translation inthe Late Twentieth Century.* Cambridge: Harvard Univ. Press.

Connolly, Claire, ed. 1999. "Postcolonial Ireland?" *European Journal of English Studies* 3 (3): 255–353.

Conrad, Kathryn, and Darryl Wordsworth. 1994. "Joyce and the Irish Body Politic: Sexuality and Colonization in *Finnegans Wake.*" *James Joyce Quarterly* 31 (3): 301–13.

Corkery, Daniel. 1931. *Synge and Anglo-Irish Literature.* Dublin: Dublin Univ. Press.

Crump, Ian. 1996. "'A Terrible Beauty Is Born': Irish Literature as a Paradigm for the Formation of Postcolonial Literatures." In *English Postcoloniality: Literatures from Around the World,* ed. Radhika Mohanram and Gita Rajan. Westport, Conn.: Greenwood Press.

Cullingford, Elizabeth Butler. 2000. "Phoenician Genealogies and Oriental Geographies: Joyce, Language, and Race." In Attridge and Howes 2000, 219–39.

Davies, Laurence. 1992. Preface to *Dubliners.* London: Wordsworth.

Deane, Seamus. 1985. *Celtic Revivals: Essays in Modern Irish Literature, 1880–1980.* London: Faber.

———. 1990. "Joyce the Irishman." In *The Cambridge Companion to James Joyce,* ed. Derek Attridge, 30–53. Cambridge: Cambridge Univ. Press.

———. 1993. "Brian Friel: The Name of the Game." In *The Achievement of Brian Friel,* ed. Alan J. Peacock, 103–12. Gerrards Cross: Colin Smythe.

———. 2000. "Dead Ends: Joyce's Finest Moments." In Attridge and Howes, 21–36.

Delaney, Frank. 1982. *James Joyce's Odyssey: A Guide to the Dublin of Ulysses.* New York: Holt, Rinehart and Winston.

Denard, Hugh. 2000. "Seamus Heaney, Colonialism, and the Cure: Sophoclean Re-Visions." *PAJ: A Journal of Performance and Art* 22 (3): 1–18.

Derrida, Jacques. 1981. "Deconstruction and the Other." In *States of Mind: Dialogues with Contemporary Continental Thinkers,* ed. Richard Kearney. Manchester: Manchester Univ. Press, 1995, 156–76.

Downing, Gregory M. 1998. "Richard Chevenix Trench andJoyce's Historical Study of Words." *Joyce Studies Annual* 9:37–68.

Driver, Felix. 1992. Geography's Empire: Histories of Geographical Knowledge. *Environment and Planning D: Society and Space* 10:23–40.

Dubino, Jeanne. 2002. "Literary Criticism Goes Global: Postcolonial Approaches to English Modernism and English Travel Writing." *Modern Fiction Studies* 48 (1): 216–26.

Duffy, Enda. 1994. *The Subaltern Ulysses.* Minneapolis: Univ. of Minnesota Press.

———. 2000. "Disappearing Dublin: *Ulysses,* Postcoloniality, and the Politics of Space." In Attridge and Howes 2000, 37–57.

Duncan, James, and Derek Gregory. 1999. Introduction to *Writes of Passage: Reading Travel Writing,* ed. James Duncan and Derek Gregory, 1–13. London: Routledge.

Eagleton, Terry. 1995. *Heathcliff and the Great Hunger: Studies in Irish Culture.* London: Verso.

Edney, Matthew. 1993. "Cartography without 'Progress': Reinterpreting the Nature and Historical Development of Mapmaking." *Cartographica,* Spring–Summer, 54–68.

———. 1997. *Mapping an Empire: The Geographical Construction of British India, 1765–1843.* Chicago: Univ. of Chicago Press.

———. 1999. "Reconsidering Enlightenment Geography and Map Making: Reconnaissance, Mapping, Archive." In *Geography and Enlightenment,* ed. David N. Livingstone and Charles W. J. Withers, 165–98. Chicago: Univ. of Chicago Press.

Ellmann, Richard. 1982. *"Ulysses" on the Liffey.* Oxford: Oxford Univ. Press.

———. 1983. *James Joyce.* Rev. ed. Oxford: Oxford Univ. Press.

Esty, Joshua D. 1999. "Excremental Postcolonialism." *Contemporary Literature* 40 (1): 22–59.

Fairhall, James. 1993. *James Joyce and the Question of History.* Cambridge: Cambridge Univ. Press.

———. 1998. "Northsiders." *European Joyce Studies* 8:43–79.

Fanon, Franz. 1963. *The Wretched of the Earth.* Trans. Constance Farrington. New York: Grove Press.

Farrelly, James P., and Mark C. Farrelly. 1998. "Ireland Facing the Voice: The Emergence of Meaninglessness in the Works of Brian Friel." *Canadian Journal of Irish Studies* 24 (1): 105–14.

Fleming, Deborah, ed. 2001. *W. B. Yeats and Postcolonialism.* West Cornwall, Conn.: Locust Hill Press.

Friel, Brian. 1981. *Translations.* New York: Samuel French.

Gaipa, Mark. 1995. "Culture, Anarchy, and the Politics of Modernist Style in Joyce's 'Oxen of the Sun.'" *Modern Fiction Studies* 41 (2): 195–217.

Gibbons, Luke. 1996. *Transformations in Irish Culture.* Cork: Cork Univ. Press in association with Field Day.

———. 2000. "'Have you no homes to go to?': Joyce and the Politics or Paralysis." In Attridge and Howes 2000, 150–71.

———. 2001. "'Where Wolfe Tone's Statue Was Not': Joyce Monuments and Memory." In *History and Memory in Modern Ireland.* ed. Ian McBride, 139–59. Cambridge: Cambridge Univ. Press.

Gibson, Andrew. 2002a. *Joyce's Revenge: History, Politics, and Aesthetics in Ulysses.* New York: Oxford Univ. Press.

———. 2002b. "Macropolitics and Micropolitics in 'Wandering Rocks.'" *European Joyce Studies* 12:27–56.

Gibson, Andrew, and Len Platt, eds. 2006. *Joyce, Ireland, Britain.* Gainesville: Univ. Press of Florida.

Gifford, Don. 1982. *Joyce Annotated: Notes for 'Dubliners' and 'A Portrait of the Artist as a Young Man.'* 2d ed. Berkeley: Univ. of California Press.

Gifford, Don, and Robert J. Seidman. 1988. *Ulysses Annotated: Notes for James Joyce's Ulysses.* New York: E. P. Dutton.

Gilbert, Stuart. 1955. *James Joyce's Ulysses.* New York: Vintage. (Orig. pub. 1930.)

———, ed. 1957–1966. *Letters of James Joyce.* New York: Viking: 1957; reissued with corrections, 1966. Vols. 2 and 3 edited by Richard Ellmann. New York: Viking Press, 1966.

Gillespie, Michael Patrick. 1986. *James Joyce's Trieste Library: A Catalogue of Materials at the Harry Ransom Humanities Research Center.* Austin: Harry Ransom Research Center.

Gjurgjan, Ljiljana Ina. 1999. "Yeats, Postcolonialism, and Turn-of-the-Century Aesthetics." *European Journal of English Studies* 3 (3): 314–26.

Glasheen, Adaline. 1977. *Third Census of "Finnegans Wake": An Index of the Characters and Their Roles.* Berkeley: Univ. of California Press.

GoGwilt, Christopher. 2000. *The Fiction of Geopolitics: Afterimages of Culture, from Wilkie Collins to Alfred Hitchcock.* Stanford: Stanford Univ. Press.

Graham, Colin. 2001. *Deconstructing Ireland: Identity, Theory, Culture.* Edinburgh: Edinburgh Univ. Press.

Grosz, Elizabeth. 1990. *Jacques Lacan: A Feminist Introduction.* London: Routledge.

Hall, Stuart. 1994. "Cultural Identity and Diaspora." In *Colonial Discourse and Postcolonial Theory: A Reader,* ed. Patrick Williams and Laura Crisman, 392–403. New York: Columbia Univ. Press.

Hardt, Michael, and Negri, Antonio. 2000. *Empire.* Cambridge, Mass.: Harvard Univ. Press.

Harris, Susan Cannon. 1998. "Invasive Procedures: Imperial Medicine and Population Control in *Ulysses* and *The Satanic Verses.*" *James Joyce Quarterly* 35 (2–3): 373–99.

Hart, Clive, and Leo Knuth. 1975. *A Topographical Guide to "Ulysses."* Colchester: Wake Newslitter Press.

Harte, Liam. 2000. "History Lessons: Postcolonialism and Seamus Deane's *Reading in the Dark.*" *Irish University Review: A Journal of Irish Studies* 30 (1): 149–62.

Haughey, Jim. 1995. "Joyce's and Trevor's Dubliners: The Legacy of Colonialism." *Studies in Short Fiction* 32 (3): 355–65.

Hawkins, Hunt. 1992. "Joyce as Colonial Writer." *College Language Association Journal* 35 (4): 301–13.

Heaney, Seamus. 1980. "The Sense of Place." In *Preoccupations: Selected Prose 1968–1978,* 131–49. New York: Farrar, Straus, Giroux.

———. 2001. "Bogland." In *Anthology of Twentieth-Century British and Irish Poetry,* ed. Keith Tuma, 657–58. Oxford: Oxford Univ. Press.

Hechter, Michael. 1975. *Internal Colonialism: The Celtic Fringe in British National Development.* Berkeley: Univ. of California Press.

Herr, Cheryl. 1991. "Ireland from the Outside." *James Joyce Quarterly* 28 (4).

Herr, Cheryl, and Chris Connell. 1993. "Political Contexts for *Ulysses,*" in *Approaches to Teaching Joyce's "Ulysses,"* ed. Kathleen McCormick and Erwin R. Steinberg, 31–41. New York: Modern Language Association.

Hofheinz, Thomas C. 1995. *Joyce and the Invention of Irish History: Finnegans Wake in Context.* Cambridge: Cambridge Univ. Press.

Holdridge, Jefferson. 2001. "An Island Once Again: The Postcolonial Aesthetics of Contemporary Irish Poetry." *Colby Quarterly* 37 (2): 189–200.

Howes, Marjorie. 2000. "'Goodbye Ireland I'm Going to Gort': Geography, Scale, and Narrating the Nation," in Attridge and Howes 2000, 58–77.

Huggan, Graham. 1994. *Territorial Disputes: Maps and Mapping Strategies in Contemporary Canadian and Australian Fiction.* Toronto: Univ. of Toronto Press.

Hutchins, Patricia. 1950. *James Joyce's Dublin.* London: Grey Walls Press.

Hyde, Douglas. 1986. *Language, Lore and Lyrics: Essays and Lectures,* ed. Breandán Ó Conaire. Blackrock: Irish Academic Press.

Innes, C. L. 2000a. "Modernism, Ireland and Empire: Yeats, Joyce, and Their Implied Audiences." In Booth and Rigby 2000, 137–55.

———. 2000b. "Postcolonial Studies and Ireland." In *Comparing Postcolonial Literatures: Dislocations,* ed. Ashok Bery, Patricia Murray, and Wilson Harris. New York: Macmillan.

Jackson, John Wyse, and McGinley, Bernard. 1995. *James Joyce's "Dubliners": An Annotated Edition.* London: Sinclair-Stevenson.

Jacoby, Russel. 1995. "Marginal Returns: The Trouble with Postcolonial Theory." *Lingua Franca,* Sept./Oct., 30–37.

Jameson, Fredric. 1984. "Postmodernism, or the Cultural Logic of Late Capitalism." *New Left Review* 146:53–92.

JanMohamed, Abdul. 1995. "The Economy of the Manichean Allegory: The Function of Racial Difference in Colonialist Literature." In Ashcroft, Griffiths, and Tiffin 1995, 18–23.

Johnson, Kerry Lee. 1997. "Vulnerable Figures: Landscape, Gender, and Postcolonial Identity in the Works of Wilson Harris, James Joyce and Jean Rhys." *DAI* 57 (12): 5143A.

Joyce, James. 1959. *The Critical Writings,* ed. Ellsworth Mason and Richard Ellmann. New York: Viking.

———. 1961. *Ulysses.* New York: The Modern Library.

———. 1966. *The Letters of James Joyce,* vols. 2 and 3, ed. Richard Ellmann. New York: Viking.

———. 1971. *Finnegans Wake.* London: Faber and Faber. (Orig. pub. 1939.)

———. 1985. *A Portrait of the Artist as a Young Man.* London: Jonathan Cape.

———. 1986. *Ulysses,* ed. Hans Walter Gabler. New York: Random House; London: Bodley Head.

———. 1993. *A Portrait of the Artist as a Young Man,* ed. R. B. Kershner. Boston: Bedford Books. (Orig. pub. 1916.)

———. 1994. *Dubliners.* Introduction by Anthony Burgess. London: Secker and Warburg. (Orig. pub. 1914.)

Kain, Richard M. 1947. *Fabulous Voyager: James Joyce's Ulysses.* New York: Viking.

Kane, Jean. 1995. "Imperial Pathologies: Medical Discourse and Drink in *Dubliners'* 'Grace.'" *Literature and Medicine* 14 (2): 191–209.

———. 1997. "National Narration and Migrant Mimicry: Restaging the Imperial Theater in Joyce and Rushdie." *DAI* 57 (8): 3507A.

Kennedy, Liam. 1996. *Colonialism, Religion and Nationalism in Ireland.* Belfast: Queen's Univ. of Belfast.

Kern, Stephen. 1983. *The Culture of Time and Space, 1880–1918.* Cambridge: Harvard Univ. Press.

Kiberd, Declan. 1996. *Inventing Ireland: The Literature of a Modern Nation.* London: Vintage.

King, Mary C. 1998. "Hermeneutics of Suspicion: Nativism, Nationalism, and the Language Question in 'Oxen of the Sun.'" *James Joyce Quarterly* 25 (3): 349–71.

Lacan, Jacques. 1977a. "Agency of the Letter in the Unconscious." In *Écrits: A Selection,* trans. Alan Sheridan, 146–78. New York: Norton.

———. 1977b. "The Freudian Unconscious and Ours." In *The Four Fundamental Concepts of Psycho-Analysis,* trans. Alan Sheridan, 17–28. New York: Norton.

———. 1977c. "The Mirror Stage as Formative of the Function of the I as Revealed in Psychoanalytic Experience." In *Écrits: A Selection,* trans. Alan Sheridan, 1–7. New York: Norton.

———. 1977d. "The Function and Field of Speech and Language in Psychoanalysis." In *Écrits: A Selection,* trans. Alan Sheridan, 30–113. New York: Norton.

———. 1977e. "The Freudian Thing, or the Meaning of the Return to Freud in Psychoanalysis." In *Écrits: A Selection,* trans. Alan Sheridan, 114–45. New York: Norton.

———. 1977f. "The Subversion of the Subject and the Dialectic of Desire in the Freudian Unconscious." In *Écrits: A Selection,* trans. Alan Sheridan, 292–325. New York: Norton.

———. 1989. *The Language of the Self: The Function of Language in Psychoanalysis,* trans. Anthony Wilden. Baltimore: Johns Hopkins Press.

———. 1993. *The Psychoses: The Seminar of Jacques Lacan, Book III, 1955–1956,* ed. Jacques-Alain Miller, trans. Russell Grigg. London: Routledge.

Law, Jules. 1999. "Political Sirens." In *Ulysses: En-gendered Perspectives,* ed. Kimberly Devlin and Marilyn Reisbaum, 150–66. Columbia: Univ. of South Carolina Press.

Lawrence, Karen. 1980. "Style and Narrative in the 'Ithaca' Chapter of Joyce's *Ulysses.*" *ELH* 47 (Autumn): 559–74.

Lerner, Daniel. 1958. *The Passing of Traditional Society: Modernizing the Middle East.* London: Free Press of Glencoe.

Lloyd, David. 1993. *Anomalous States: Irish Writing and the Post-Colonial Moment.* Durham: Duke Univ. Press; Dublin: Lilliput Press.

———. 1999. *Ireland After History.* Field Day Essays. Cork: Cork Univ. Press.

———. 2000. "Counterparts: *Dubliners,* Masculinity, and Temperance Nationalism." In Attridge and Howes 2000, 128–49.

———. 2001. "Regarding Ireland in a Post-Colonial Frame." *Cultural Studies* 15 (1): 12–32.

Loomba, Ania. 1998. *Colonialism/Postcolonialism.* London: Routledge.

Lyotard, Jean-Françoise. 1992. "Answer to the Question, What Is the Postmodern?" In *The Postmodern Explained: Correspondence 1982–1985,* trans. Don Barry, Bernadette Maher, Julian Pefanis, Virginia Spark, and Morgan Thoma, 1–16. Minnesota: Univ. of Minnesota Press.

Macauley, Thomas. 1995. "Minute on Indian Education." In Ashcroft, Griffiths, Tiffin 1995, 428–30. (Orig. pub. in *Speeches of Lord Macauley with his Minute on Indian Education,* selected with an introduction and notes by G. M. Young. Oxford: Oxford Univ. Press.)

MacCabe, Colin. 1985. *Theoretical Essays: Film, Linguistics, Literature.* Manchester: Manchester Univ. Press.

———. 2003. *James Joyce and the Revolution of the Word.* 2d ed. New York: Palgrave Macmillan.

Mackinder, Halford. 1902. *Britain and the British Seas.* New York: D. Appleton.

Maguire, Peter A. 1999. "*Finnegans Wake* and Irish Historical Memory." *Journal of Modern Literature* 22 (2): 293–327.

Mahaffey, Vicki. 1998. *States of Desire: Wilde, Yeats, Joyce, and the Irish Experiment.* New York: Oxford Univ. Press.

Mahan, Alfred Thayer. 1905. *The Influence of Sea Power upon History, 1660–1783.* 19th ed. Boston: Little, Brown.

Mahony, Christina Hunt. 1996. "Poetry in Modern Ireland: Where Postcolonial and Postmodern Part Ways." *Comparatist: Journal of the Southern Comparative Literature Association* 20:82–92.

Majumdar, Saikat. 2007. "Desiring the Metropolis: The Anti-Aesthetic and Semicolonial Modernism." *Postcolonial Text* 3 (1): 1–14.

Maley, Willy. 2000. "'Kilt by Kelt Shell Kithagain with Kinagain': Joyce and Scotland." In Attridge and Howes 2000, 201–18.

Malinowski, Bronislaw. 1984. *Argonauts of the Western Pacific.* Prospect Heights, Ill.: Waveland. (Orig. pub. 1922.)

Malouf, Michael. 1999. "Forging the Nation: James Joyce and the Celtic Tiger." *Jouvert: A Journal of Postcolonial Studies* 4 (1): 29.

Maloy, Kelli Elizabeth. 1999. "'Out of the Shambles of Our History': Irish Women and (Post)Colonial Identity." *DAI* 60 (6): 2039A.

Manganaro, Marc. 2002. *Culture, 1922: The Emergence of a Concept.* Princeton: Princeton Univ. Press.

Manganiello, Dominic. *Joyce's Politics.* Boston: Routledge and Kegan Paul, 1980.

Martin-Iordache, Corina. 2002. "Modernism, Postcolonialism, and the Experience of Place: A Study of Samuel Beckett and Derek Walcott." *DAI* 63 (6): 2232A–33A.

Marx, Karl, and Frederick Engels. 1972. *Ireland and the Irish Question,* ed. R. Dixon. New York: International Publishers.

Matthew, H. C. G., and Morgan, Kenneth O. 1992. *The Oxford History of Britain: The Modern Age,* vol. 5. Oxford: Oxford Univ. Press.

Mays, Michael. 1998. "*Finnegans Wake,* Colonial Nonsense, and Postcolonial History." *College Literature* 25 (3): 20–34.

———. 2005. "A Nation Once Again? The Dislocations and Displacements of Irish National Memory." *Nineteenth Century Contexts* 27 (2): 119–38.

McClintock, Anne. 1992. "The Angel of Progress: Pitfalls of the Term 'Post-Colonialism.'" *Social Text* 31/32.

McGee, Patrick. 2001. *Joyce Beyond Marx: History and Desire in "Ulysses" and "Finnegans Wake."* Gainesville: Univ. Press of Florida.

McGrath, F. C. 1999. *Brian Friel's (Post)Colonial Drama: Language, Illusion, and Politics.* Syracuse: Syracuse Univ. Press.

McHugh, Roland. 1991. *Annotations to Finnegans Wake.* Rev. ed. Baltimore: Johns Hopkins Univ. Press.

McVeagh, John, ed. 1996. *Irish Travel Writing: A Bibliography.* Dublin: Merlin Publishing.

Meche, Jude R. 2000. "'A Country that Called Itself His': Molloy and Beckett's Estranged Relationship with Ireland." *Colby Library Quarterly* 36 (3): 226–41.

Mezey, Jason Howard. 1999. "Ireland, Europe, The World, The Universe: Political Geography in *A Portrait of the Artist as a Young Man.*" *Journal of Modern Literature* 22 (2): 337–48.

Mikics, David. 1990. "History and the Rhetoric of the Artist in 'Aeolus.'" *James Joyce Quarterly* 27 (3): 533–55.

Molino, Michael R., ed. 1996. "Postcolonial Theory and Irish Literature." *Comparatist: Journal of the Southern Comparative Literature Association* 20:41–92.

Moloney, Caitríona, and Helen Thompson. 2000. "Introduction: 'Border Traffic.'" *Journal of Commonwealth and Postcolonial Studies* 7 (1): 3–14.

Moloney, Caitríona, Helen Thompson, and Frederick Sanders, eds. 2000. "Ireland as Postcolonial." *Journal of Commonwealth and Postcolonial Studies* 7 (1): 1–168.

Moore, Seán. 2000. "'Anglo-Irish' Hybridity: Problems in Miscegenation, Representation, and Postcolonialism in Irish Studies." *Journal of Commonwealth and Postcolonial Studies* 7 (1): 75–110.

Moore-Gilbert, B. 1997. *Postcolonial Theory: Contexts, Practices, Politics.* London: Verso.

Mottolese, William. 2002. "'Wandering Rocks' as Ethnography? Or Ethnography on the Rocks." *James Joyce Quarterly* 39 (2).

Mullin, Katherine. 2000. "Don't Cry for Me, Argentina: 'Eveline' and the Seductions of Emigration Propaganda." In Attridge and Howes 2000, 172–200.

Murphy, Sean Patrick. 1999. "James Joyce and the Logic of Victimage." *DAI* 60 (6): 2040A.

Nash, John. 2000. "'Hanging Over the Bloody Paper': Newspapers and Imperialism in *Ulysses.*" In Booth and Rigby 2000, 175–96.

Ní Fhlathúin, Máire. 2000. "The Anti-Colonial Modernism of Patrick Pearse." In Booth and Rigby 2000, 156–74.

Nolan, Emer. 1995. *James Joyce and Nationalism.* London: Routledge.

———. 2000. "State of the Art: Joyce and Postcolonialism." In Attridge and Howes 2000, 78–95.

O'Brien, Eugene. 1998. *The Question of Irish Identity in the Writings of William Butler Yeats and James Joyce.* Lewiston, N.Y.: Edward Mellen Press.

———. 1999. "Alternate Islands: Emigration and the Epistemology of Irish Identity." *Jouvert: A Journal of Postcolonial Studies* 4 (1): 40.

———. 2000. "Anastomosis, Attenuations and Manichean Allegories: Seamus Heaney and the Complexities of Ireland." *Journal of Commonwealth and Postcolonial Studies* 7 (1): 51–73.

———. 2003. *Seamus Heaney and the Place of Writing.* Gainesville: Univ. Press of Florida.

O'Connor, Theresa. 1996. "History, Gender, and the Postcolonial Condition: Julia O'Faolain's Comic Rewriting of *Finnegans Wake.*" In *The Comic Tradition in Irish Women Writers,* 124–48. Gainesville: Univ. Press of Florida.

O'Leary, Timothy. 2000. "Putting Ireland on the Postcolonial Map: Brian Friel's Translations." *New Literatures Review* 37:27–41.

Osteen, Mark. 1995. *The Economy of "Ulysses": Making Both Ends Meet.* Syracuse: Syracuse Univ. Press.

Pearce, Richard, ed. 1994. *Molly Blooms: A Polylogue on 'Penelope' and Cultural Studies.* Madison: Univ. of Wisconsin Press, 1994.

Pearl, Cyril. 1969. *Dublin in Bloomtime: The City James Joyce Knew.* New York: Viking Press.

Pearson, Nels C. 2001. "'Outside of Here It's Death': Co-Dependency and the Ghosts of Decolonization in Beckett's *Endgame.*" *ELH* 68 (1): 215–39.

———. 2002. "Fictions of Exile: The Irish Expatriate in Europe and the Postcolonial Dimensions of Modernism, 1914–1960." *DAI* 62 (12): 4179A.

Pelan, Rebecca. 2000. "Antagonisms: Revisionism, Postcolonialism and Feminism in Ireland." *Journal of Commonwealth and Postcolonial Studies* 7 (1): 127–47.

Pierce, David. 1992. *James Joyce's Ireland.* New Haven, Conn.: Yale Univ. Press.

———. 1998. "The Politics of *Finnegans Wake.*" *Textual Practice* 2 (3): 367–80.

Pine, Richard. 1999. *The Diviner: The Art of Brian Friel.* 2d ed. Dublin: Univ. College of Dublin Press.

Pordzik, Ralph. 2001. "A Postcolonial View of Ireland and the Irish Conflict in Anglo-Irish Utopian Literature since the Nineteenth Century." *Irish Studies Review* 9 (3): 331–46.

Porter, Dennis. 1993. "Modernism and the Dream of Travel." In *Literature and Travel.* Rodopi Perspectives on Modern Literature 11, ed. Michael Hanne, 53–70. Amsterdam: Rodopi.

Pratt, Mary Louise. 1986. "Fieldwork in Common Places." In *Writing Culture,* ed. James Clifford and George E. Marcus, 27–50. Berkeley: Univ. of California Press.

———. 1992. *Imperial Eyes: Travel Writing and Transculturation.* London: Routledge.

Prince, Gerald. 1987. *A Dictionary of Narratology.* Lincoln: Univ. of Nebraska Press.

Ragland-Sullivan, Ellie. 1986. *Jacques Lacan and the Philosophy of Psychoanalysis.* London: Croom Helm.

Ramazani, Jahan. 1998. "Is Yeats a Postcolonial Poet?" *Raritan: A Quarterly Review* 17 (3): 64–89.

Regan, Stephen. 2000. "Poetry and Nation: W. B. Yeats." In *Literature and Nation: Britain and India,* ed. Richard Allen and Harish Trivedi, 78–94. London: Routledge/Open Univ.

Richards, Thomas. 1993. *The Imperial Archive: Knowledge and the Fantasy of Empire.* London: Verso Press.

Riquelme, J. P. 1998. "Location and Home in Beckett, Bhabha, Fanon, and Heidegger." *Centennial Review* 42 (3): 541–68.

Roche, Anthony, ed. 2006. *The Cambridge Companion to Brian Friel.* Cambridge: Cambridge Univ. Press.

Rushdie, Salman. 1991. *Midnight's Children.* New York: Penguin Books.

———. 1992. *Imaginary Homelands: Essays and Criticism 1981–1991.* New York: Penguin Books.

Said, Edward. 1978. *Orientalism.* New York: Pantheon.

———. 1988. *Nationalism, Colonialism and Literature: Yeats and Decolonization.* Derry: Field Day.

———. 1990. "Yeats and Decolonization." In *Nationalism, Colonialism, and Literature,* 69–95. Minneapolis: Univ. of Minnesota Press.

———. 1992. *Imaginary Homelands: Essays in Criticism, 1981–1991.* New York: Penguin Books.

———. 1994. *Culture and Imperialism.* New York: Vintage Press.

Sarup, Madan. 1992. *Jacques Lacan.* Hemel Hempsted: Harvester Wheatsheaf.

Schwarze, Tracey Teets. 1997. "Silencing Stephen: Colonial Pathologies in Victorian Dublin." *Twentieth Century Literature* 43 (3): 243–63.

Seidel, Michael. 1976. *Epic Geography: James Joyce's "Ulysses."* Princeton, N.J.: Princeton Univ. Press.

Senn, Fritz. 1995. *Inductive Scrutinies: Focus on Joyce.* ed. Christine O'Neill. Baltimore: Johns Hopkins Univ. Press.

Sharma, Shailja. 2001. "Salman Rushdie: The Ambivalence of Migrancy." *Twentieth Century Literature* 47:596–620.

Sidorsky, David. 2001. "The Historical Novel as the Denial of History: From 'Nestor' via the 'Vico Road' to the Commodious Vicus of Recirculation." *New Literary History* 32 (2): 301–26.

Smyth, Gerry. 1995. "The Past, the Post, and the Utterly Changed: Intellectual Responsibility and Irish Cultural Criticism." *Irish Studies Review* 10:25–29.

Song, Chae-pyong. 1999. "Re-Narrating the Nation at (Post)Colonial Moments: Cultural Politics and Critical Nationalists in Joyce, O'Brien, and Rushdie." *DAI* 60 (1): 143A.

Spivak, Gayatri Chakravorty. 1985. "Can the Subaltern Speak?: Speculations on Widow Sacrifice." *Wedge* 7 (8): 120–30.

Spurr, David. 1996. "Writing in the *Wake* of Empire." *MLN* 111 (5): 872–88.

———. 2002. *Joyce and the Scene of Modernity.* Gainesville: Univ. Press of Florida.

Stocking, George W., Jr. 1992. "Maclay, Kubary, Malinowski: Archetypes from the Dreamtime of Anthropology" in *The Ethnographer's Magic and Other Essays in the History of Anthropology,* 212–17. Madison: Univ. of Wisconsin Press.

Thompson, Frederick Diodati. 1893. *In the Track of the Sun; or, Readings from the Diary of a Globe-Trotter.* New York: D. Appleton.

Tindall, William York. 1969. *A Reader's Guide to Finnegans Wake.* New York: Farrar, Straus, and Giroux.

Tratner, Michael. 1995. *Modernism and Mass Politics: Joyce, Woolf, Eliot, Yeats.* Stanford: Stanford Univ. Press.

Tymoczko, Maria. 1994. *The Irish Ulysses.* Berkeley: Univ. of California Press.

Ungar, Andras. 2002. *Joyce's Ulysses as National Epic: Epic Mimesis and the Political History of the Nation State.* Gainesville: Univ. Press of Florida.

Valente, Joseph. 1995. *James Joyce and the Problem of Justice: Negotiating Sexual and Colonial Difference.* Cambridge: Cambridge Univ. Press.

———. 1998. "Between Resistance and Complicity: Metro-Colonial Tactics in Joyce's *Dubliners.*" *Narrative* 6 (3): 325–40.

———. 2000. "'Neither Fish Nor Flesh'; or How 'Cyclops' Stages the Double-bind of Irish Manhood." In Attridge and Howes 2000, 96–127.

Van Boheemen-Saaf, Christine. 1999a. "Epiphany and Postcolonial Affect." In *Moments of Moment: Aspects of the Literary Epiphany,* ed. Wim Tigges. Amsterdam: Rodopi.

———. 1999b. *Joyce, Derrida, Lacan, and the Trauma of History: Reading, Narrative, and Postcolonialism.* Cambridge: Cambridge Univ. Press.

Van Boheemen-Saaf, Christine, and Colleen Lamos, eds. 2001. *Masculinities in Joyce: Postcolonial Constructions.* Amsterdam: Rodopi.

Watson, G. J. 1987. "The Politics of *Ulysses.*" In *Joyce's Ulysses: The Larger Perspective,* ed. Robert D. Newman and Weldon Thornton, 39–58. Newark: Univ. of Delaware Press.

Whelan, Kevin. 2002. "The Memories of 'The Dead.'" *Yale Journal of Criticism* 15 (1): 59–97.

Wicht, Wolfgang. 2000. "'And That Now Was How It Was': Politics of Memory in James Joyce's *Ulysses.*" *Symbolism: An International Journal of Critical Aesthetics,* 1: 233–51.

Williams, Trevor L. 1996. "'Brothers of the Great White Lodge': Joyce and the Critique of Imperialism." *James Joyce Quarterly* 33 (3): 377–97.

———. 1997. *Reading Joyce Politically.* Gainesville: Univ. Press of Florida.

Wilson, A. N. 2002. *The Victorians.* London: Hutchinson.

Wolleager, Mark A., Victor Luftig, and Robert Spoo, eds. 1996. *Joyce and the Subject of History.* Ann Arbor: Univ. of Michigan Press.

Yeats, W. B. 1997. "Ireland and the Arts." In *The Yeats Reader,* ed. Richard J. Finneran, 364–68. New York: Scribner Poetry.

Index

Note: Italic page number indicates an illustration. Fictional and mythological characters are indicated by (fict.) after the uninverted name.